6⁵⁰

The Heart of Beethoven

The Heart of Beethoven

Selden Rodman   James Kearns

SHOREWOOD PUBLISHING CO., INC., NEW YORK

BOOKS BY SELDEN RODMAN

VERSE

The Amazing Year
The Revolutionists
The Airmen
Lawrence: The Last Crusade
Mortal Triumph and Other Poems

ART

The Insiders
Conversations with Artists
The Eye of Man
Portrait of the Artist as an American
Renaissance in Haiti
Horace Pippin: A Negro Painter in America

MUSIC

The Heart of Beethoven

TRAVEL

Mexican Journal: The Conquerors Conquered
Haiti: The Black Republic

ANTHOLOGIES

One Hundred Modern Poems
One Hundred American Poems
War and the Poet (with Richard Eberhart)
The Poetry of Flight
A New Anthology of Modern Poetry

To
Jean Brinkema

J. K. S. R.
Betty Leonora

True originality consists not in being different from others, but in being wholly in harmony with oneself.

—GUSTAV ERNEST

It is the peculiarity of Beethoven that he can use the words 'best' and 'noblest' without making an intelligent man laugh up his sleeve . . . The very words 'good,' 'noble,' 'spiritual,' 'sublime,' have all become in our time synonymous with humbug. In Beethoven's music they take on a new and tremendous significance and not all the corrosive acid of the most powerful intellect and the profoundest skepticism can burn through them into any leaden substratum. They are gold throughout.

—W. J. TURNER

It is the peculiarity of Beethoven's imagination that again and again he lifts us to a height from which we must revaluate not only all music but all life, all emotion, and all thought.

—ERNEST NEWMAN

Beethoven the man and Beethoven the composer are not two unconnected entities, and the known history of the man may be used to throw light upon the character of his music.

—J. W. N. SULLIVAN

Beethoven was of all men the last to tolerate the belief that the artist has a temperament which sets him above the standards of ordinary citizenship, or excuses his failure to reach them. Whatever his sins may have been (and on this subject the evidence is doubtful), he was eminently a man who held himself responsible. Joachim once remarked of a clever French musical critic that 'this Parisian shows no sense for the great penitent that there was in Beethoven.' Beethoven was far too busy to torment himself, but Joachim was profoundly right about his penitence. It was a quality that was, if possible, more out of fashion in Beethoven's time than it is now. But it will always be inseparable from responsibility so long as human beings have ideals and fail to reach them.

—D. F. TOVEY

Contents

Overture

BEETHOVEN's heart, noble and affirmative throughout the dissonant passage of his fifty-seven years, sends out its impulses to other hearts more piercingly today than it ever did when Beethoven lived. Life is short and art is long, as we all know, but only in music are there no barriers set up by time; no burdens of creed, costume, language; no mysteries of iconography; no national colors or ideological passwords. In the music of Beethoven, this miracle of communication is manifested man-to-man as well as artist-to-artist—and in an apparently ever-widening crescendo.

Was this phenomenon destined to end where it began? Is it to diminish the genius of Brahms, Wolf, Strauss, Sibelius, Stravinsky, Webern, and others who have followed in Beethoven's wake, to suggest that each in his way was inhibited by the prototype and contributed to the growing separation between "professional" and "popular"? Did the completeness with which Beethoven sounded the depths of every form. he mastered insure this? Is all art now doomed to such division? Or is something to be learned from an exploration of the relation between this artist's life and his art?

Beethoven arrived on the scene when the art of music in the West had completed its novitiate as the handmaiden of religious and courtly observance. It was free for the first time to express the whole range of human emotions. And Beethoven himself from the first seems to have felt that this was to be his destiny. Between naked feeling and form—he tells us in a variety of ways—there must be identity. The bridge is constructed by the discipline of the active intellect. The new departs gradually from what has been firmly established. There isn't a word about how to "modulate" in Beethoven's writings and talk—though modulation is his metaphor.

The *message* is what matters. It was no caprice that Beethoven admired above all his predecessors a composer who took the same view. "My lord," Handel once reproved a patron who had complimented him on the "noble entertainment" offered by *The Messiah*, "I should be sorry if I only entertained them. I wish to make them better." Listen to Beethoven brush aside Czerny's suggestion that he composes for fame or to solve a problem: "Nonsense! . . . What weighs on my heart must come out, and that's why I've written!" Or again, speaking frankly to Naegeli during the turbulent years devoted to the Mass in D: "My chief object was to awaken, and deeply impress, religious feelings both on singers and hearers." Leonard Bernstein, at the end of a spirited dialogue in *The Joy of Music*, calls this obsession with content our sense of the music's "inevitability":

L. B.:
Form is only an empty word, a shell, without this gift of inevitability; a composer can write a string of perfectly molded sonata-allegro movements, with every rule obeyed, and still suffer from bad form. Beethoven broke all the rules, and turned out pieces of breath-taking rightness . . . *Something is right in the world. There is something that checks throughout, that follows its own law consistently: something we can trust, that will never let us down.*

L. P.:
But that is almost a definition of God.

L. B.:
I meant it to be.

THREE BEETHOVENS

The traditional three periods into which Beethoven's music (and therefore his life) falls correspond with the cycles of human experience. In the First Period, the young man masters the conventions of the world as he finds it, and in so doing dares to defy them. The *Pathétique* of 1798 and other early piano sonatas, rather than the more conventional symphonies and string quartets preceding 1803, may be regarded as the characteristic works of this period, for in them Beethoven elected to express his protest against the Eighteenth Century's acceptance of social inequality.

In the Second Period, this mood of defiance is pitted against a growing awareness that evil will not yield to mere force, that suffering is every man's lot. The issue is always in doubt, and there is the drama. Since this unresolved awareness corresponds to maturity, insofar as most people ever mature, the music through which Beethoven gave voice to it constitutes his most popular. The heroic élan of the Fifth Symphony has in it the quality of being all things to all men. E. M. Forster put it this way in *Howard's End:*

It is generally admitted that Beethoven's Fifth Symphony is the most sublime noise that has ever penetrated into the ear of man. All sorts and conditions are satisfied by it. Whether you are like Mrs. Munt and tap surreptitiously when the tunes come—of course so as not to disturb the others—or like Helen, who can see heroes and shipwrecks in the music's flood; or like Margaret, who can only see the music; or like Tibby, who is profoundly versed in counterpoint and holds the full score upon his knee; or like their cousin, Fraulein

14

Mosebach, who remembers all the time that Beethoven is "echt Deutsch"; or like Fraulein Mosebach's young man, who can remember nothing but Fraulein Mosebach; in any case the passion of your life becomes more vivid, and you are bound to admit that such a noise is cheap at two shillings.

In this music, in the less compact but more personal Third Symphony, and in the opera *Fidelio* which occupied Beethoven throughout his middle phase and which he loved above all his works for the pain it cost him, Beethoven's subject is freedom. How it feels to have it; what it means to be without it; the exaltation and the desperation; the wind murmuring in the trees and the forward rush of undammed water; the birds in their limitless kingdom, and Leonora throwing herself upon Florestan to receive Pizarro's knife before her lover. The willingness to sacrifice one's life for something more meaningful is weighed, balanced, weighed again; and so is the cost—*but not the responsibility before God*—that was to come later. Yet Beethoven, who never left anything to chance, was beginning to explore this imponderable by composing simultaneously works less singleminded in their import. The Third and Fifth Symphonies and the "Appassionata" Sonata are far from comprising the whole burden of his Second Period. The "Rasoumovsky" quartets, the song cycle *An die ferne Geliebte* and the Seventh Symphony are peaks rising at least as high, offering in the ascent vistas of thought and feeling more extraordinary if less spectacular.

If, following the *Lebewohl* Sonata and the "Harp" Quartet of 1809, Beethoven had not written another note, he would remain among the most universally appealing of artists. But Beethoven's most profound music was still to be written. The works of his Third Period, though enjoyable to many—as they were not in Beethoven's lifetime—are comprehensible only in the context of a spiritual experience few undergo and no artist but Beethoven ever wholly expressed.

Hints of what was to come are perceptible in the introduction to the third "Rasoumovsky" quartet, and throughout the darkly chromatic F Minor Quartet of 1810—but it is doubtful whether Beethoven as late as 1814 knew where sound would lead him. The music of that year seemed to be collapsing in bombast. In two years he was to write nothing; in four, very little. Deafness, which had been closing in on him since his twenty-eighth year, was now complete. His nephew—on the impossible feat of whose upbringing as a paragon of virtue Beethoven had staked the emotional savings of a dozen unrequited loves—would soon seek to take his own life. Beethoven's once powerful frame was wracked by diseases for which there was then no cure. He sensed that death itself could not be much longer postponed. As an artist what was there left for him to do?

Should he take flight to London where his fame was legendary and the promise of wealth, even for the slightest of efforts, beckoned? Had he made a mistake in throwing General Kyd out of his lodgings because that patron of the arts asked for a symphony in his early manner? He wanted money desperately for his nephew; he knew he could have it if he repeated (with variations, of course) any of the triumphant performances the world accepted and loved. "There is no salvation," he wrote in his diary, "except to go away, only by that can you lift yourself up to the summits of your art again, while here you are sinking into vulgarity . . ." The temptations—especially the temptation to fall back upon a *style,* letting the *content* take care of itself, as in the music of his own generation and most of the arts of every age—were enormous.

MUSIC AS THERAPY

Had Beethoven in 1815 countered his impulse to escape the responsibilities of his miserable situation by merely shutting the world out and analyzing his private nightmare, musicologists might have had ciphers to decode for centuries. But the most uplifting music ever to stir human beings would have remained unwritten. Sketches for the Ninth Symphony are to be found on pages surrounding the passage quoted from his diary. But the key to incorporating them in a communicable structure was still missing. We are indebted to Mendelssohn for a clue to its discovery. The A Major Sonata completed in 1816, first of the characteristic works of the Third Period, is dedicated to the pianist Dorothea Ertmann. Long after Beethoven's death the aged Baroness told how in the months preceding the writing of this sonata she had lost her last child and was on the verge of what we now call a nervous breakdown. Hearing of this, Beethoven invited her to his rooms. When she arrived, he said: "We will now talk to each other in tones," and he improvised on his piano for more than an hour—something he hadn't done in years. "He told me everything," she confided to Mendelssohn, "and at last brought me comfort."

In the sonata growing out of this experiment in psychic therapy, Beethoven discoursed for the first time at length about a resolution he had begun to grope for in words as far back as 1812. Letters and diaries of that year include the following: "Alone, alone, alone! . . ."; "Submission, absolute submission to your fate . . ."; "You may no longer be a man, not for yourself, only for others . . ."; "O God, give me strength to conquer myself . . ." Could a way be found of concluding such a discourse without renouncing the world, forgetting others' salvation in the pursuit of one's own?

Sebastian Bach, most profoundly religious of Protestant artists, had found the many-voiced fugue ideally suited to expressing mortal aspiration. Beethoven, whose personal interpretation of Catholicism surges with Protestant overtones, had been from earliest youth unique among his contemporaries in his devotion to the forgotten master of Leipzig. Contrapuntal passages are not infrequent among the works of Beethoven's Second Period, but the composer now prepared to make an elaborate fugue the very climax of Dorothea Ertmann's sonata.

By this means would the content of succeeding major works achieve an ultimate dimension. At the very least, as in the awesomely experimental *Hammerklavier* Sonata that was to follow, the fugues would explore the terrors and complexities of the search. At their best they would celebrate with joy the transfiguration of finite but aspiring man into infinite Godhead.

Since Beethoven's creative spirit never rejects anything (and therefore loses nothing), we should not be surprised to find him returning again and again to the springs of youth. The *Pathétique's* uprising violence was not to be confined to the prideful malaise and heady salon-storming of the composer's first days in Vienna. In the Second Period it is ever-present, generally as the Dionysian protagonist in a tense duel between convulsion and order, but sometimes triumphant still, as in the shattering conclusion to the "Appassionata" Sonata. Even in the Third Period, as in the opening pages of the last sonata, its thunders (now heaven-storming) are no less imperious for having been transferred from mortal to Olympian hands. Nor are the unearthly resolutions that follow reserved for those prepared for a like submission; they may be cherished for their celestial beauty alone.

"IN MY END IS MY BEGINNING"

Beethoven's life, as truly as any creator's, was the source of his art. What he made, he was—though not vice versa. The life, so contradictory, so humanly fallible, so often "failing" in the conflict between ideals and performance, yielded in the act of creation to a will that refused to settle for less than triumphant (and finally transcendant) conclusions.

Everyone who knew Beethoven remarked his lack of sophistication. There was no guile in him, no histrionic posing. His aims in life were as other men's: a wife and children, many friends, a steady income, good food and wine, nature, travel, puns, practical jokes. Writing to a friend at the time he was completing his last quartet, he explained: "If I ever let the muse sleep, it is only that she may awaken the stronger. I hope still to bring some great works into the world, and then, like an old child, to end my earthly career among good men . . ."

An old child . . . Beethoven never lost his capacity for wide-eyed wonder. Was this gift granted him because "true" childhood had been denied? Was it because his naturally out-going nature had experienced suffering so early that its ultimate expression could only take the form of joy? Was this what Beethoven had in mind when he said that anyone who truly grasped the import of his music would be "absolved from all the misery that bows down other men"?

Let us see.

18

From
Bonn
to
Heiligenstadt

1770-1802

THE SOUND OF BELLS

At six in the morning of January 15, 1777, the carillon in the clock tower of the Electoral Palace at Bonn began to play the overture to *The Deserter* by Pierre Alexandre Monsigny, a French composer of light operas. The tune was never finished. A fire which had broken out three hours earlier in a distant wing reached the powder magazine. The tower caught fire and crumbled and the bells crashed to the ground.

How many echoes are in that crash! Beethoven, seven years old at the time, was not too young to be affected by them. His terrified father, the Court music-master, who was already drilling the little boy to be a lucrative prodigy of the keyboard like Mozart ten years before, rushed his family to the banks of the Rhine as the fire swept through the town unchecked. Court Councillor Von Breuning, whose widow and children were to become the composer's earliest friends, died a hero's death in the flames.

The revolution that was to sweep through Europe and the world was still a decade away. Its prophets were busy, but the Old Order was resisting their subversion with no visible signs of alarm in its stately ritual. The Old Order in music seemed hardier still. Mozart's genius, and Haydn's, guided divertimento and minuet over the rippling courses of the Alberti bass with a serenity that seemed impervious to fiery concussion.

But the sound of that arrested ringing was never to be forgotten by Beethoven. He would choose his lodgings for the rest of his life near churches, hearing the vibrations from their towers when everything else audible mocked him with its stillness. He would keep bells of silver and clay on his desk always. And in the finales to *Fidelio* and the Ninth Symphony strains of Monsigny's forgotten opera would ring once more, and forever.

GROWING UP IN BONN

Cäcilie Fischer, the landlord's sister in the Beethovens' new house by the Rhine, was to remember "the tiny boy, standing on a footstool in front of the clavier to which the implacable severity of his father so early condemned him," and a friend of the Fischers at this same time used to see him standing there "weeping." Franz Wegeler, Beethoven's lifelong friend, who would be less inclined to melodramatize the worst moments, reports only looking occasionally from his own backyard into the Beethovens' and observing the "doings and sufferings" of his playmate.

Beethoven's grandfather, a distinguished *Kapellmeister* and citizen of parts, died in 1773. But long before his death he had withdrawn in dignity from the affairs of his ambitious but hopelessly self-indulgent son. He had disapproved of Johann van Beethoven's marriage to Maria Magdalena Laym, widow of a valet and daughter of a cook. He disapproved of his son's heavy drinking, making no allowances for the fact that alcoholism ran in the family. He must have disapproved of Johann's indifferent musicianship. But whether he would have frowned upon the exploitation of his obviously talented little grandson, there is no way of guessing beyond the veneration with which the composer was always known to speak of him. Very likely his snobbish attitude toward Frau Beethoven would have given him little authority to interfere.

Two years after the great fire in the palace Beethoven's father got help in his pedagogic labors. Tobias Pfeiffer, Court tenor by profession, is said to have been a good pianist; but whether this had any effect in confirming the future composer's taste for this instrument among the many to which he was haphazardly being subjected, we don't know. Pfeiffer survives in history only for his share in the most notorious legend of Beethoven's childhood. "Often," the story goes, "when he came with Beethoven the father from the winehouse late at night, the boy was roused from his sleep and kept at the pianoforte until morning."

Sullivan, at the risk of seeming heartless, puts these early trials of Beethoven in musical perspective: "From the point of view of Beethoven's development he had what can only be regarded as favorable surroundings in his early years. They were undesirable, as his deafness was calamitous, only from the point of view of his personal happiness. From the point of view of mankind at large they were advantages." Who is to say how much the sensitive boy suffered, or what he would have become had he been treated with understanding from the start? Did his schoolmates nickname him "The Spaniard" merely because his complexion was swarthy, or because his features were already beginning to assume the lowering look of one who fortifies his resistance to a cruel environment with the only weapon at his command—pride? The musicologist Paul Bekker, commenting on the childhood compositions of the Bonn days, observes that the second of the three little

24

sonatas dedicated to the Elector Maximilian Friedrich reveals "a knowledge of suffering appalling in a twelve-year-old boy."

What were Beethoven's father and mother really like? We can only guess. Psychoanalysts (to whom we shall refer later) have gone to great lengths to "prove" that Beethoven's "rejection" of his father for denying him the "normal" love he might have received, conditioned him for the abnormal "fatherly" anxiety he was later to exercise upon his unfortunate nephew. Johann Beethoven, sober, was probably a kindly parent. Consciously, at least, Beethoven was to bear him no grudge. With that sense of loyalty that never left him, young Ludwig was once seen "furiously interposing to rescue his drunken father from an officer of the police." It was remarked years later that the composer—though he never brought up the subject of his father, or made any reference to his death in 1792—refused to countenance any derogatory references to him. Nevertheless it is not far-fetched to suppose that the spirit of revolt that burned in Beethoven throughout his life caught fire from opposition to a father's arbitrary tyranny.

How different was Beethoven's relationship to his mother. The only words surviving from her mouth tell a great deal about her own pathetic existence. "What is marriage?" she asked Cäcilie Fischer. "A little joy followed by a chain of sorrows." The sorrows began when her first husband, a valet, died young. They continued when *Kapellmeister* Beethoven refused to attend her second wedding. The first child of this union lived only six days. Of six others, only three survived. No wonder Maria Magdalena was never seen to laugh and was described as sometimes "hot-tempered and quarrelsome." Her peasant background makes it certain that she carried little weight in family decisions, and this gives some support to the conjecture that Beethoven's feelings toward her may have been ambivalent. Yet the evidence of her compassion for her son's early miseries is incontrovertible. She was the first of the many shields of love that were to stand between him and the adoption of a defensive cynicism. She accompanied Ludwig on an abortive performing-trip down the Rhine into Holland when he was eleven and the only thing we know about it is that she warmed his feet in her lap one cold night. She died of tuberculosis in 1787 and Beethoven's earliest surviving letter testifies to the depth of his loss: "Who was happier than I when I could still utter the sweet name of mother, and heed was paid to it; and to whom can I say it now? to the dumb pictures resembling her, the creations of my imagination?"

Beethoven was more fortunate with the piano teacher who followed Pfeiffer. Christian Gottlob Neefe was a fine musician; and the description of his thirteen-year-old pupil which he wrote in the third-person for an English musical journal is remarkable.

Louis van Beethoven . . . a boy of eleven [Father Johann had falsified his son's birth records for exploitative purposes] and of most promising talent . . . plays the clavier very skilfully and with power, reads at sight very well, and—to put it in a nutshell—he plays chiefly *The Well-Tempered Clavier* of Sebastian Bach, which Herr Neefe put into his hands. Whoever knows this collection of preludes and fugues in all the keys—which might almost be called the *non plus ultra* of our art—will know what this means. So far as his duties permitted, Herr Neefe has also given him instruction in thorough-bass. He is now training him in composition and for his encouragement has had nine variations for the pianoforte written by him on a march—by Ernst Christolph Dressler—engraved at Mannheim. This youthful genius is deserving of help to enable him to travel.

Beethoven's general education was inevitably neglected. But does it matter that he never learned to spell (even the name of Haydn!), to write elegantly, to get the product of five times seventeen without writing seventeen out five times and reaching the result by addition? "His whole education has been neglected," a friend was later to note, "and apart from his art he is coarse, but honest and unaffected; he says quite bluntly whatever he may be thinking. Great thoughts drift through his soul but he cannot express them in any form but in music." It is not to be inferred from this that Beethoven was unfamiliar with great literature or that his respect for every branch of knowledge was less than overwhelming. The arts and science, he was to tell Bettina Brentano, are paths leading to the same higher realm. Now he was reading Klopstock with the passion he was later to confer upon Shakespeare and Goethe. Among his books when he died were Plutarch, Cicero, and Kant's *Theory of the Heavens*. "You will not easily find a treatise," he wrote his publishers in 1809, "that is too learned for me; without laying claim to any genuine learning, I yet accustomed myself from childhood onward to grasp the spirit of the best and wisest in every age. Shame on the artist who does not consider it his duty to achieve at least as much."

But the future composer profited most from the musical atmosphere of the Electoral Court itself. The time was coming to an end when a provincial European capital of less than ten-thousand inhabitants could be an intellectual center and testing-ground for all that was unfamiliar in the arts of its time. Such a microcosm was Bonn. The Elector Max Franz, like all the children of the Empress Maria Theresa, was a performing musician and disregarded social rank where art was concerned. Concerts of sacred and profane works, involving voices and every conceivable combination of instruments, were nightly affairs. The gaiety was constant and the excitement frequent. New plays by Lessing, Voltaire, Beaumarchais, Goldoni, Garrick, and later Schiller and Goethe, were staged. Operas, grand and comic, were imported from Italy and France. To the familiar names, the rising stars of Gluck, Mozart and Haydn were added with approval. And in all these activities the young Beethoven participated.

Beethoven's friendships during the final years at Bonn played as decisive a role in shaping his character as anything derived from study and music-making. How pallid a thing has friendship become today—especially among men. From our proximity to the English public school system, perhaps, we associate any such deep feelings, at least if expressed, with effeminacy. Beethoven's early letters to his friends, especially those to Franz Wegeler and Karl Amenda, who were to stay close to his heart as long as he lived, are rapturous. Here is the first to Wegeler:

In what an odious light have you exhibited me to myself! Oh! I acknowledge it, I do not deserve your friendship. It was no intentional or deliberate malice that induced me to act toward you as I did—but inexcusable thoughtlessness alone.

I say no more. I am coming to throw myself into your arms, and to entreat you to restore me my lost friend; and you will give him back to me, to your penitent, loving, ever grateful

BEETHOVEN.

And to Amenda:

The *best man I ever knew* has a thousand times recurred to my thoughts! Two persons alone once possessed my whole love, one of whom still lives, and you are now the third. How can my remembrance of you ever fade?

In literature the Romantic movement was already well under way. Who can say whether Beethoven's habit of thus unburdening his heart to all he loved wasn't preparing him for such initial musical expressions of rapture as the Largo of the D Major piano sonata?

"There was never a time," Wegeler was to write in his memoirs half a century

later, "when Beethoven was not in love, and that in the highest degree." In Bonn, Beethoven's relationships with women were probably still platonic; at least they left no scars. Eleanora von Breuning, daughter of the heroic Court Councillor, played a disquieting role. For one thing she was his pupil, and Beethoven's relations with pupils were never happy. For another, she was a member of the aristocratic family that had virtually adopted him. (The "van" in Beethoven's name had no nobility-conferring derivation.) To have declared himself a suitor would have been lacking in tact and gratitude. Stephan von Breuning, Eleanora's brother, was already a dear friend, and their mother—who tolerated his moods by declaring "Beethoven is in a 'raptus' again!"—had already come too close to replacing his mother in his affections to be antagonized. There are indications that Beethoven was unhappy in this restraint, and his correspondence with "Lorchen" establishes the patter of affection-grievance-reconciliation that was to typify so many later friendships. Once, when she had sent him an embroidered scarf as a peace offering, he wrote:

> Your magnanimous behavior fills me with shame. . . . If only you could have seen how this incident affected me yesterday you would certainly not accuse me of exaggeration if I now say to you that your token of remembrance caused me to weep.

And then he adds, pointedly, "Farewell, my friend; for it is impossible for me to give you any other name." Eleanora von Breuning became the wife of Wegeler later on; but Beethoven's romantic attachment to her may have survived in the name of the heroine of *Fidelio*. In one early letter he addresses her "Most Estimable Leonora!"

EVE OF DEPARTURE

In 1792 Beethoven made up his mind to leave Bonn for Vienna. He was twenty-two. His parents and two brothers no longer required his support. His chores as organist, viola player in the Court orchestra, and teacher of piano, left him little time to compose. He had played for Mozart once, in 1787, but in 1791 this great artist died. Haydn had visited Bonn several times and had already seen enough of the scowling young man's work to be impressed. Haydn, who had recognized the infant Mozart's genius instantly, now recognized Beethoven's. His secure position as the world's most eminent living musician did not prevent him from thus generously recommending the obscure Beethoven to the Elector of Cologne:

I humbly take the liberty of sending Your Serene Electoral Highness some musical works, viz., a Quintet, an eight-part Parthie, an oboe Concerto, variations for the forte-piano, and a Fugue, compositions of my dear pupil Beethoven. . . . Connoisseurs and non-connoisseurs must candidly admit, from these present pieces, that Beethoven will in time fill the role of one of Europe's greatest composers.

Beethoven never took the job in Cologne, but he followed the aging Master to Vienna. He admired immensely the aloof perfection of Haydn's style without in any way desiring to imitate it. But he knew that before he could give effective voice to his own more tempestuous feelings, he had much to learn; and who could better teach him? The music-lovers of Bonn were already at his feet—especially when he improvised—but who were the music-lovers of Bonn? Would the professionals in the world's music capital be as easily moved? Might he not be suffering from delusions of grandeur?

His friends were writing generous sentiments in an album to be presented to him on his departure. Count Waldstein, for whom he had "ghosted" a ballet score, wrote: "With the help of assiduous labor you shall receive Mozart's spirit from Haydn's hands." Flatterers all. . . . The Old Order was indeed crumbling. The French Revolution was rolling toward complacent Germany like an avalanche. Refugees were already pouring into Bonn ahead of the advancing *sans culotte*

32

armies. . . . Yet Bonn, the Electoral Court, the aristocracy, Papa Haydn, all had been good to him, and believed (as no other society on earth) *in music*. Conflict, as always, raged in Beethoven's soul. He leaned over and added these lines of his own to the album:

> I am not wicked—fiery blood
> Is all my malice, and my crime is youth.
> Wicked I am not, truly I am not wicked;
> Though wild upsurgings often may plead against my heart,
> My heart is good.—
> To help wherever one can,
> Love liberty above all things,
> Never deny the truth
> Even at the foot of the throne!

FIRST DAYS IN VIENNA

When Beethoven, arriving in Vienna in November of 1792, had had several sessions with Haydn, he asked the old man for a frank estimate of his character. "You strike me," Haydn wisely replied, "as a man who has several heads, several hearts, and several souls." Haydn was not pleased by his twenty-two-year-old pupil's head-strong nature, and he offended Beethoven by remarking that he would be well advised to withdraw one of the three Trios in his Opus 1. Beethoven, of course, thought it was the best one. Yet Haydn had been right in sensing the essential duality of the young composer. At this stage of his career Beethoven was more interested in

electrifying a gathering by his unparalleled talent for improvising at the keyboard than he was in writing music "according to the book." When he did commit his thought to paper, as in the Mozartean Trios, or in the first three piano sonatas of Opus 2 (which he dedicated—with a touch of sarcasm?—to "Mr. Joseph Haydn, Doctor of Music"), or in the earlier works in many forms which he did not care to publish, he stuck fairly closely to the accepted forms.

In a sense, Beethoven was to do this always. But later on he was to find ways of revolutionizing the forms from within, the better to convey their content, holding together what seemed to be free modulations by a systematic progression in the bass. Presently he had not found that way, and being instinctively too fine an artist to do violence to the forms themselves, he preferred to let go emotionally in his playing. Mozart in his C Minor sonata (K. 457) had started off with a rising sequence of notes out of the tonic chord. Beethoven begins his first sonata with the same progression, only substituting for Mozart's characteristically ornamented resolution a mildly rebellious fillip of his own. (There is a resemblance to the finale of Mozart's E Minor Symphony here, too.) The younger artist's personality erupts more dramatically in the second sonata; the first three movements are beyond Mozart's or Haydn's range; one is in the Eighteenth Century for the first thirty-one measures of the rondo, and then—for just seven bars—a characteristic turbulence threatens to break loose before Beethoven pulls the piece together and resumes the mask he still frequently elects to wear. Further expressions of personality would have to wait. Consummate beauty, departing a little but a very little from what had gone before, was the aim (and the attainment) of the Trios, the first six string-quartets of Opus 18, the Septet in E-flat Major (Opus 20), the first two concertos and symphonies. Only in the piano sonatas, and even there step by step until he reaches the Largo already mentioned and the passionate outbreak of the *Pathétique,* is the voice of the other Beethoven, the insistently expressive Beethoven, clearly heard. (Only the very early sonatas that bear the misleading opus number 49 are wholly Mozartean).

Meanwhile, he was playing, and improvising, without restraint. What was his playing like? What effect did it have on the salons where he was in growing demand? And how was he affected by this adulation? There is a revealing description of his appearance at this time. It is from the pen of a young pianist.

His attire was very ordinary and far removed from the choiceness customary in those days, and particularly in our circles. Besides, he spoke in a pronounced dialect and had a rather common way of expressing himself. . . . I still remember distinctly how both Haydn and Salieri sat on a sofa on one side of the little music-room, both most carefully dressed in the old-fashioned style, with bagwig, shoes and silk stockings, while Beethoven used to appear even here in the freer ultra-Rhenish garb, almost carelessly dressed.

Beethoven was already applying the style of revolution to the social level; he was beginning to revolutionize the attitude of the artist to society—and of society to the artist. Haydn, who now referred to him as "Our Great Mogul," was offended perhaps more by Beethoven's unconventional conduct than by his stormy piano style. But the aristocracy was not. The musical nobles may have been amused by the young genius' boorish ways, but they were also impressed—and a little awed. Wegeler, fleeing the revolutionary vanguard that had now surged over Bonn, was amazed to note the self-confidence of his once-shy friend. Prince Lichnowsky, at whose town-house Beethoven was now visiting, quickly discovered that his guest could not be treated as Mozart and Haydn had been. After a sharp exchange or two, Beethoven's habit of arriving for meals when he felt like it received no further comment. The Prince instructed his valet to answer Beethoven's summonses first. And when he offered Beethoven the use of his horse, the haughty young man promptly declined and hired his own. Lobkowitz, another princely patron who gave Beethoven his small orchestra to experiment with and whom Beethoven sometimes called Fitzli-Putzli, was made to pay in humility for even suggesting that Beethoven was not the peer of Handel and Goethe. "With men who will not believe and trust in me because I am not yet famous," Beethoven rebuked him, "I can hold no intercourse." Publishers were treated more high-handedly. Close friends, like Barons Zmeskall von Domanovecz and Gleichenstein, were flattered to be the butt of the flamboyant pianist's puns. Only handsome women and old men received any tokens of deference.

Was Beethoven becoming arrogant? Had the first tastes of success and power gone to his head? Momentarily, perhaps. "I don't want any of your moralizing," he wrote "Baron Mucksplasher" (Zmeskall) in a joking letter. "Strength is the morality of those who stand out from the rest, and it is mine." It is well to remind oneself at this point that Beethoven for the moment was alone in recognizing his composing mastery. The world-mood of revolt against feudal authority, moreover,

36

demanded expression through *personality*: Beethoven always had to *live* what his emotions impelled him to create. But one should also reflect that had Beethoven succumbed to this mood he would have become at worst a travelling virtuoso, at best advancing no further in his art than the torrential cataract of the "Moonlight" Sonata's *presto agitato*.

EARLY TRIUMPHS

"Courage!" Beethoven wrote in his diary of 1795. "Even with all the frailties of my body, my spirit shall dominate. Twenty-five years have come: this year must decide the mature man. Nothing must remain." But in the five exuberant years that were to follow there are few signs that Beethoven gave much thought to this gloomily prophetic foreboding. His health appeared to be excellent. His first popular success in composition, the song *Adelaïde,* was published in 1797. Musically he was maturing only in the sense of learning to adapt the old forms more freely, and of building a formidable backlog of skills. Though already a competent violinist, he now took lessons from Krumphölz. When he had learned what Haydn had to teach him—he scoffed unfairly that he had learned nothing—he received correction in his exercises in counterpoint from Johann Schenck. Then he subjected himself to the grueling pedantry of J. G. Albrechtsberger, master of Catholic ritual music. He did not reply to friends who wondered what possible use this "archaic" tradition could be to one bent upon getting ahead in "modern art." He proceeded to Mozart's operatic rival, Salieri, for instruction in the matching of vocal music and texts. Mozart himself—parts of whose A Major Quartet (K. 464) Beethoven copied out while at work on his own A Major (Opus 18, No. 5)—was probably the best "teacher" of all.

Concurrently, of course, Beethoven continued to be lionized for his performing talents, basking in the glamor of the salons, writing occasional sonatas and sets of variations that suitably called upon the resources of his manual wizardry. Glimpses of this side of him have come down. Czerny tells us that no one equalled Beethoven "in rapidity of scales, double trills, skips" and that he used both pedals frequently. "His hands were densely covered with hair and the short fingers, especially at the tips, were very broad. When playing his demeanor was masterfully quiet, noble and beautiful, without the slightest grimace—only bent forward low, as his deafness grew upon him." The piano as we know it was just coming into general use, receiving its sixth octave during Beethoven's first years in Vienna, and Beethoven exploited its novel dynamics to the full. Another contemporary pianist compared his improvising to the celebrated Abt Vogler's: "Bethofen [sic] in addition to the execution, has greater clearness and weight of ideas, and more expressiveness —in short, he is more for the heart—equally great, therefore, as an *adagio* or *allegro* player."

Every commentator on Beethoven has paused to speculate over the story of his improvising one of his audiences into a state of audible sobbing and then turning harshly upon them from the keyboard with uproarious laughter and calling them fools. Tovey's comment carries most weight:

> Now this may be impish, but it is not Mephistophelean. It is an outward sign of one of the highest qualities of Beethoven's spiritual grace. In a more conciliatory form, it is represented by William James' profound observation that it is not good for us to be content to enjoy art passively, and that, if we cannot ourselves be artists, we must at all events not receive without giving; so that, for instance, it would be a good thing for every non-musician who has enjoyed a great musical experience to follow it by being kind to his aunt or doing some similar act of disinterested duty. It is a fundamental principle with Beethoven that not only tragedy and comedy, but beatific visions and common daylight, are inextricably mingled.

The French Revolution which by this time (to quote Tovey again) "had shaken the foundations of aristocracy all over the world too thoroughly to allow the further musical development of Mozart's exquisite irony," was now reaching Vienna in its physical aspect. Had Beethoven already found ways of expressing tragic themes without an Eighteenth Century twist? Assuredly he had. The two romantic sonatas of 1801 which he had labelled *quasi una fantasia* to underscore their departure from inorganic rigidity, were proof enough of that. But it must be said before proceeding further that Beethoven never surrendered himself to Romanticism. It was not in his nature to surrender. If Classicism be defined as the tendency to control emotion and impose order on creation then Beethoven was throughout his career a classicist. What he had discovered now, and even before this, was how to give voice to romantic moods, convulsive emotion, anguish, without sacrificing form, without changing direction, without losing his relentless grip on reality, without losing sight for one instant of the ultimate destination implicit in an initial commanding proclamation. "Beethoven's rhythm and phrasing are simpler than Haydn's and very much simpler than Mozart's, just because his dramatic and harmonic expression has an enormously larger range," Tovey observes.

But what Beethoven also had not found at this juncture was a theme broad enough to encompass those outward changes in the world that reflected his youthful inner turmoil. The architecture in which to fittingly house such an epic did not yet exist. The arrival of the French in Vienna supplied him with the first of these needs.

Beethoven's political status in the Imperial capital had been ambiguous from the outset. On the one hand he was the darling of the nobility; he must have recognized, at least dimly, what is now so obvious to us: that never before or since has a society devoted to one of the arts so lavished its gifts on a worthy artist. On the other hand Beethoven's republican sentiments were well known. The Emperor would have nothing to do with him, and probably tolerated his presence in the capital only because the Archduke Rudolph, who was his pupil, idolized him. When General Bernadotte, the commander of Bonaparte's vanguard, established himself in the French Embassy, Beethoven was probably the only prominent inhabitant of the city who dared to be seen hobnobbing with him socially. Bernadotte was not insensible to the honor—or to the opportunity. He had brought with him a team of artists and intellectuals and it was their mission to proselytize for the new ideology. Bernadotte could, and did, suggest tactfully that a major composition on the symbolism of the revolutionary hero's victories would meet with a handsome reception in Paris and even be repaid with the First Consul's favor. Beethoven, who must already have thrilled to the humanitarian pronouncements that accompanied the Italian Campaign, and been impressed with Bonaparte's capacity to bring order out of the Terror, responded readily. He was already making sketches for a work of similar heroic content, he told Bernadotte—an overture and incidental music to a ballet on the Prometheus theme. Prometheus had brought fire to men and now Bonaparte was using that fire to free them! There were also plans for a sonata in A-flat Major. One can imagine the conversation concluding somewhat as follows:

BERNADOTTE: —likewise celebrating a great man?

BEETHOVEN: Well, not exactly, General. But I do plan to include in it a funeral march on the death of a hero.

BERNADOTTE: (*smiling urbanely*) Let us not talk of *death*, my dear Beethoven!

BEETHOVEN: A great many people are dying. Even heroes must die sooner or later. The fortunate die while they are still heroes.

BERNADOTTE: You Germans take such gloomy views of history!

BEETHOVEN: General, *this* funeral march isn't going to be gloomy. It will be sombre, but martial. I even intend to give it some drum rolls and a cannon-shot or two! (He laughs uproariously and strides to the piano). Like this!

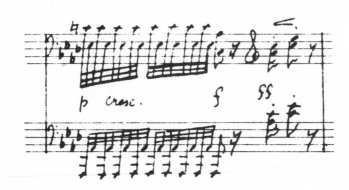

BERNADOTTE: I like that.

BEETHOVEN: I thought you would.

BERNADOTTE: You're making fun of me?

BEETHOVEN: Each to his taste, General. But tell me, what is General Bonaparte's taste in music? Monsieur Kreutzer won't say, if he knows.

BERNADOTTE: (*smiling*) He likes a rousing tune; but I've seen him nod during some of the heavier numbers. At a performance of Chevalier Gluck's "Orfée" for example.

BEETHOVEN: Hm. The best things make the biggest people nod, even in our society.

BERNADOTTE: I can guarantee one thing, that the First Consul will be pleased by the outcome of our conversation yesterday, the new symphony you plan to write—

BEETHOVEN: (*slyly*) Because its subject will be his career?

BERNADOTTE: (*Gallicly*) Let us say, rather— because it will have been composed by the most ardent of his subjects!

The theme—man's will to free himself and others, whatever the cost in suffering— was ready-made. Thus far Bonaparte's career seemed to exemplify the triumphs of such a hero. But what of the means of expressing such a subject? Beethoven had acquired the technical capacities by now, but technical capacities can only serve to project what one has experienced. Beethoven had experienced triumphs, triumphs

40

as resounding in the realm of art as Bonaparte's in his realm. But had he known suffering?

The dreadful answer to this question came crowding upon him so insistently that for a time the idea of a Bonaparte symphony was quite forgotten. In fact it was all that the young composer could do to keep his sanity by composing, as if in a trance, music that said nothing but Yes! over and over again to the receding vision of untroubled beauty.

THE SOUND OF SILENCE

For three years now Beethoven had been mildly disturbed by a ringing in his ears. He had confided this only to doctors, and the doctors had prescribed contradictory remedies. These brought him no relief. Some time in the spring of 1801 it came over him that he was destined to be deaf. Letters to Amenda and Wegeler contain the burden of fears which at last became too nerve-wracking to bear alone. For once Beethoven's self-confidence deserts him. The letter to Amenda, then living in Latvia, must be quoted in full:

How often do I wish you were with me, for your Beethoven is living an unhappy life, quarrelling with nature and its creator, often cursing the latter because he surrenders his creatures to the merest accident, which can break or destroy the most beautiful blossoms. Know that my noblest faculty, my hearing, has greatly deteriorated. When you were still with me I felt the symptoms but kept quiet; now it is continually growing worse, and whether or not a cure is possible has become a question; but it is said to be due to my bowels, and so far as they are concerned I am nearly restored to health. I hope indeed that my hearing will also improve, but I am dubious because such diseases are often incurable. . . .

Oh, how happy I would be if my hearing were completely restored; then would I hurry to you, but as it is I must refrain from everything, and the most beautiful years of my life must pass without accomplishment of the promise my talent and powers hold. I must resort to a sad resignation, although I am resolved to rise superior to every obstacle. But how will that be possible? Yes, Amenda, if in six months' time my malady shows itself to be incurable, I shall appeal to you; you must abandon everything and come to me. My affliction stands least in my way of playing and composing, most in conversation with others, and you must be my companion. I am sure fortune will not desert me. What might I not attempt? Since you went away I have written in every form except opera and church music. You will not deny me; you will help your friend bear his cares and affliction.—I have received all your letters, and in spite of having answered so few, I have you always in mind and my heart beats for you as ever. I beg of you to keep secret what I have told you about my deafness and *confide it to nobody, no matter who it is.*

42

Now farewell, my dear, good fellow; if you think I can do something for you here, command me as a matter of course.

Your faithful and truly affectionate

L. v. Beethoven

To Wegeler, Beethoven opens more obliquely. First he talks of their childhood in Bonn and his feelings of loss at their separation, concluding proudly: "I want to say that you will see me again only as a great man." Then, dropping his defenses, he comes to the point:

My ears ring and buzz continually, day and night. I am living a wretched life; for two years I have avoided almost all social gatherings because it is impossible for me to tell people—"I am deaf." If I belonged to any other profession it would be easier, but in mine it is an awful situation, the more so because of my enemies, and they are not few. —What would they say? . . . I have often cursed my existence; Plutarch taught me resignation. If possible I will bid defiance to my fate, although there will be moments in my life when I shall be the unhappiest of God's creatures. . . . If my condition continues I will go to you next spring; you could hire a house for me in some pretty place in the country and for half a year I would be a farmer. This might bring about a change. Resignation! What a wretched refuge—and yet it is the only one open to me.

Wegeler invited Beethoven to visit with him and Lorchen in Bonn, but Beethoven declined:

Do not believe that I could be happy with you. What is there that could make me happier? Even your care would give me pain. I would see pity on your faces every minute, and be still more unhappy. . . . Oh, if I were rid of this affliction I could embrace the world! I feel that my youth is just beginning, and have I not always been ill . . .? No! I cannot endure it. I will take fate by the throat; it shall not overcome me. Oh, it is so beautiful to live—to live a thousand times! I feel that I was not made for a quiet life.

A year passed during which Beethoven gave every outward indication of indeed living "a thousand times." He returned to the social life of Vienna, concealing his affliction. He "took fate by the throat," cutting in on the melancholy *Adagio* of his B-flat Major Quartet with snatches of cavorting *Allegro*. He spoke no more of "resignation." He wrote Wegeler of "a dear, bewitching girl who loves me and whom I love." He joked, quarrelled and made up with his day-to-day companions, as always.

Only Wegeler knew the bitter truth. The "dear, bewitching girl" for whom he had felt "for the first time" the possibility of "happiness in marriage," was in all probability Giulietta Guiccardi, a flirtatious belle to whom he had dedicated the second of those *fantasia* sonatas, the already-popular "Moonlight." "Alas!" he wrote Wegeler, "she is not of my station—and now—it would be impossible for me to marry." Obviously. Who would want to marry an eccentric, "ugly" musician, doomed to total deafness? Who, least of all a 'teen-age darling of the Viennese *haute monde*, would want to spend the prime of her life writing questions on a slate while he shouted (he was already, like all deaf people, conscious of straining his voice) exasperated answers?

But the full measure of Beethoven's despair in that thirty-first summer of his life would never have been known had not a document, intended only for his brothers after death, been found among his papers in 1827. He had been staying at Heiligenstadt, a sylvan suburb, on doctors' orders. Friends who dropped by observed him wandering the fields, as he always did, or composing industriously at his desk. Only young Ferdinand Ries noticed anything unusual:

At times, at 8 o'clock in the morning after breakfast he would say: "Let us first take a short walk." We went and frequently did not return until 3 or 4 o'clock, after having made a meal in some village. On one of these wanderings . . . I called his attention to a shepherd who was piping very agreeably in the woods on a flute made of a twig of elder. For half an hour Beethoven could hear nothing, and though I assured him that it was the same with me (which was not the case), he seemed extremely quiet and morose. When occasionally he seemed to be merry it was generally to the extreme of boisterousness; but this happened seldom.

It was the boisterousness of a soldier on the eve of a fateful battle. It was the moroseness of one contemplating the lost opportunities of a short life. It was the quiet that comes over a man when he knows he has only a matter of hours in which to discover the meaning of everything past and to come. Beethoven was contemplating death:

You men who think or say that I am malevolent, stubborn, or misanthropic, how greatly do you wrong me, you do not know the secret causes of my seeming so, from childhood my heart and mind were inclined to gentleness and goodwill, I was always eager to accomplish great deeds, but reflect now that I have been in a wretched condition aggravated by senseless doctors, while year after year I was deceived in my hopes of improvement, and finally faced with the prospect of a *lasting malady* (whose cure may take years or turn out to be impossible); born with an ardent and lively temperament, even susceptible to the diversions of society, I was compelled early to keep apart, to live in loneliness; when at times I tried to live this down, O how harshly was I defeated by the doubly tragic experience of my bad hearing, and yet I could not say to people, speak louder, shout, for I am deaf. Ah, how could I possibly admit an infirmity in the *one sense* which should have been more acute in me than in others, a sense which I once possessed in highest perfection, a perfection such as surely few in my profession enjoy or have ever enjoyed —O, I cannot do it, therefore forgive me when you see me draw back when I would gladly mingle with you, my misfortune is doubly painful because it must lead to my being misunderstood, for me there can be no refreshment from association with my fellows, no subtle intercourse, no ready flow and exchange of thoughts, only the barest needs of communication will be allowed me in society, I must live like an exile, if I come near people a hot terror seizes me, a fear that my condition may be noticed—so it has been during the half year I have been spending in the country, as ordered by my intelligent physician that my hearing might be spared as much as possible, this was in accord with my inclinations, although I sometimes longed for society, but what a humiliation when one stood beside me and heard a flute in the distance, and *I heard nothing*, or someone heard a *shepherd singing*, and again I heard nothing, such incidents brought me almost to despair. I almost reached the point of putting an end to my life—only art it was that held me back, ah, it seemed impossible to leave the world until I had brought forth all that I felt called upon to produce, and so I endured this wretched existence—truly wretched, a sensitive body which a sudden change can throw from the best into the worst state—Patience—that is what I must now choose for my guide, I have done so, may my determination endure until it pleases the inexorable Parcae to break the thread, perhaps I shall get better, perhaps not—I am prepared. Forced already in my 28th year to become a philosopher, O, it is not easy, and harder for an artist than another—God, thou lookest into my inmost being, Thou knowest that love of man and desire to do good live in me. O men, when some day you read these words, reflect that you did me wrong, may I in my misfortune be consoled by finding one of my kind who, despite all obstacles of nature yet did all that was in his power to be accepted among worthy artists and men. You my brothers Carl and [The omission here and in the address of Brother Johann's name has never been explained] as soon as I am dead if Dr. Schmid is still alive ask him in my name to describe my malady and attach this written sheet to the history of my illness so that so far as is possible the world may become reconciled with me after death. At the same time I declare you two to be the heirs of my small fortune (if so it can be called), divide it fairly, bear with and help each other, what injury you have done me you know has long been forgiven. To you brother Carl I give special thanks for the attachment you have shown toward me of late. It is my wish that your lives may be better and freer from care than I have had, recommend *virtue* to your children, it alone can give happiness, not money, I speak from experience, it was virtue that upheld me in misery, to it next to my art I owe the fact that I did not end my life by my own hand—Farewell and love each other—I thank all my friends, particularly Prince Lichnowsky and Professor Schmidt—I desire that the instruments from Prince L. be preserved by one of you but let no quarrel result from this, as soon as they serve you to no better purpose sell them, how glad will I be if I can still be helpful to you in my grave—with joy I hasten toward death— if it comes before I have had an opportunity to show all my artistic capacities it will still come too early for me despite my hard fate and I shall probably wish that it had come later—but even then I am satisfied, will it not free me from a state of endless suffering? Come when thou wilt, I shall meet thee bravely—Farewell and do not wholly forget me when I am dead, I deserve this of you, for I have in life often thought of how to make you happy, be so—

Ludwig van Beethoven
[Black Seal]

Heiglnstadt [sic]   *October 6, 1802*

So do I take my farewell of you—and indeed sadly—yes, that beloved hope—which I brought with me when I came here to be cured at least in some degree—I must wholly abandon it, as the leaves of autumn fall and are withered, so hope has been blighted, almost as I came I go away—even the high courage—which often inspired me in the beautiful days of summer—has disappeared—O God—grant me at last but one day of pure joy— it is so long since real joy has echoed in my heart—O when—O when—O Divine One— shall I feel it again in the temple of nature and of men—Never? No—O that would be too hard.

One day of pure joy? Was Beethoven trying in this most pathetic, incoherent, agonized of confessions to deceive his brothers, his prospective mourners, and the world? He who had written in these very weeks some of the most joyful music ever to delight a long-faced world? The full-bodied summer strains of his Second Symphony lying on the same desk, complete and scarcely dry; the notebooks brimming with the lighthearted trills of the G and E-flat Major sonatas; whom was he trying to fool?

Of course he was fooling no one—nor trying to. The tumbling words of this alien medium rush too compulsively for that. Certainly he was not saying that deafness of itself, even total deafness, could be any obstacle to his *composing,* for who could know better than he that sounds, like thoughts, course through the echoing silences of the mind's "ear" more gloriously than in any rocking auditorium? What was he trying to say, then? Was he trying to say that the artist is first of all a man, a man who must come to terms with life and other men before he can ever "create" anything worth creating? In his own case that he must come to terms with this new (and forever) fact of aloneness, and indeed make a virtue of it, rising above pride, above his vanity as a performer, rising even above any hope of what he still most hoped for: a normal domestic life?

And in the music on that desk was he saying that art before it can fulfill its highest function—giving joy out of suffering—must express the quintessence of unalloyed exuberance?

And finally was he saying that only now, if and when he found the courage to survive as a man, would he be ready as an artist to undertake the expression of a true hero's odyssey: the aspirations, defeats, resurrections and ultimate victories of a conqueror worthy to stand among the gods?

A conqueror who had conquered himself:

The
Years
of
Triumph

1803-1812

ON THE BRINK

If the Heiligenstadt Testament stands at the first great divide in Beethoven's life, bringing the curtain down on his youth and ushering in the prodigious decade of his prime, the music immediately surrounding that event serves to dramatize the cleavage. The Second Symphony, composed at Heiligenstadt, while it could not have been written by Mozart or Haydn, belongs to the Eighteenth Century. In its musical resources it sums up the best these great composers had to offer symphonically, adding only enough of the decisive touch of Beethoven's personality through its orchestral coloration to remove it absolutely from the category of a work of imitation. In its spirit it sums up what Karl Pidoll has a disillusioned old man say about the age the Revolution guillotined forever: "The man of the eighteenth century, in his best and truly representative form, possessed what the present age lacks in such depressing measure—nobleness of mind. He knew respect, but not fear. He knew pride, but not vanity. He knew freedom but not license, he knew power but not despotism; he knew the terrible adversities of Fate, but he also knew his own capacity for making light of them. He knew all this at the very last as an ideal, and he believed this ideal to be attainable, both for the individual and for mankind as a whole."

EROICA

The Third Symphony, begun immediately after Heiligenstadt, is not only inconceivable as an expression of eighteenth century man—though Beethoven himself was never to lose his grip on any of the qualities mentioned by Pidoll—it represents in art one of the greatest single expressive leaps forward ever accomplished.

Napoleon!—That such a work could ever have been associated with such a little man seems incredible. Yet it was. The association could not possibly have lasted. Beethoven's own recognition of the absurdity of it was bound to become a legend. Ferdinand Ries and Prince Moritz Lichnowsky both claim to have witnessed the scene. Here is Ries's account:

In this symphony Beethoven had Buonaparte in his mind, but as he was when he was First Consul. Beethoven esteemed him greatly at the time and likened him to the greatest Roman consuls. I as well as several of his more intimate friends saw a copy of the score lying upon his table, with the word "Buonaparte" at the extreme top of the title-page and at the extreme bottom "Luigi van Beethoven" but not another word. Whether, and with

what the space between was to be filled out, I do not know. I was the first to bring him the intelligence that Buonaparte had proclaimed himself emperor, whereupon he flew into a rage and cried out: "Is then he, too, nothing more than an ordinary human being? Now he, too, will trample on all the rights of man and indulge only his ambition. He will exalt himself above all others, become a tyrant!" Beethoven went to the table, took hold of the title-page by the top, tore it in two and threw it on the floor. The first page was rewritten and only then did the symphony receive the title: "Sinfonia eroica."

Thayer, who saw a manuscript, says that one of the two words erased was

"Bonaparte" and that just under his own name Beethoven had written with a lead pencil in large letters, nearly obliterated but still legible, "Composed on Bonaparte."

Ries has left a fascinating account of the first rehearsal of the *Eroica:*

> In the first Allegro occurs a wicked whim (*böse Laune*) of Beethoven's for the horn; in the second part, several measures before the theme recurs in its entirety, Beethoven has the horn suggest it at a place where the two violins are still holding a second chord. To one unfamiliar with the score this must always sound as if the horn player had made a miscount and entered at the wrong place. At the first rehearsal of the symphony, which was horrible, but at which the horn player made his entry correctly, I stood beside Beethoven, and, thinking that a blunder had been made I said: "Can't the damned hornist count?—it sounds infamously false!" I think I came pretty close to receiving a box on the ear. Beethoven did not forgive the slip for a long time.

Many have described just what is revolutionary in the construction of this most revolutionary of masterpieces. A pianist once proposed to write a treatise on nothing more than the musical-psychological significance of the two harsh bursts that precede the statement of the opening theme. That bugle-call

has been identified as a version of the Prometheus ballet theme already referred to as having been written two years before. One of the devices that gives the symphony its unprecedented unity is that this Prometheus motif, in different guises, appears

in the other three movements as well. But the theme has still earlier antecedents. It happens to correspond with the opening of the twelve-year-old Mozart's operetta, *Bastien et Bastienne.*

Tribute, forgotten memory, or coincidence? Schauffler points out that while the second subject of the *Eroica's* Scherzo is a variant of the initial "Hero" theme, the Scherzo's first subject is a syncopated version of the second subject of the first movement! The ramifications are endless. I mention a few only to emphasize the interlocking complexity of the work and to suggest that when Beethoven was seized by it he called up, unconsciously no doubt, all the resources of his vast musical memory. The opening phrase of the symphony, Burk writes:

. . . is on its face value an insignificant figure on the common chord. But no sooner was it defined than the mind, totally possessed, began to build and reach. The exposition is a mighty projection of 155 bars, music of concentrated force, wide in dynamic and emotional range, conceived apparently in one great stretch, where the pencil could hardly keep pace with the outpouring thoughts. . . . There are no periodic tunes here, but fragments of massive chords, and sinuous rhythms, subtly articulated but inextricable, meaningless as such except in their context. Every bar bears the heroic stamp. There is no melody in the conventional sense, but in its own sense the music is melody unbroken, in long ebb and flow, vital in every part. Even before the development is reached the composer has taken us through mountains and valleys, shown us the range, the universality of his subject. The development is still more incredible as it extends the classical idea of a brief thematic interplay into a section of 250 bars. It discloses vaster scenery in which the foregoing elements are newly revealed, in their turn generating others. The recapitulation (beginning with the famous passage in which the horns mysteriously sound the returning tonic E flat against a lingering dominant chord) restates the themes in the increased strength and beauty of fully developed acquaintance. But still the story is not told. In an unprecedented coda of 140 bars, the much exploited theme and its satellites reappear in fresh guise, as if the artist's faculty of imaginative growth could never expend itself. . . .

Burk's description elsewhere of the general significance of the four movements is equally perceptive:

The idealized heroism of the *Eroica,* music of profound and personal experience, could have been nothing else than autobiographical. The heroism is Beethoven's own indomitable spirit extended and universalized. In the first movement it is the heroism of intrepidity, where faith and strength become one, a strength which exalts and purifies. The funeral march soon ceases to be elegiac. Its solemnity has no odor of mortality; death has no place in Beethoven's thoughts as an artist. The spirit which gathers and rises in the middle portion sweeps inaction aside and becomes life assertion even more penetrating than that in the long crescendos and shattering chords of the opening movement. These two

56

movements are the movements of conquering. The last two are clear and confident—the *Scherzo* serene, the *Finale* joyous. The shouting triumph of the close has no tramp of heavy, crushing feet. It is a jubilant exhortation to all mankind, a foreshadowing of the finales of the Fifth and Ninth Symphonies. . . . No man on this earth could have fitted the dimensions of the *Eroica*—none save the artist who wrote it. . . .

In the *Eroica* Beethoven had only begun to act upon his new conception of music as the triumphant liberator of man from his sorrows. The years from its completion in 1804 to the completion of the Eighth Symphony in 1812, the most prolific of Beethoven's life, were given over to this grand design. Five symphonies, not counting the Third; the "Waldstein" and "Appassionata" Sonatas; the two finest piano concertos and the Violin Concerto; *Fidelio*; all the major trios and songs; and the three "Rasoumovsky" Quartets—these comprise no more than the peaks of an unrivalled eight-years' elevation.

But it would be wrong to assume that Beethoven was now spending all of his time, or even most of it, bent over a desk. If there were no other proof, the out-going music of this Second Period would itself give the lie to any such possibility. Once come to terms (he was never to be reconciled) with his deafness, Beethoven threw himself daemonically into social-musical ventures, new friendships, many loves.

APPASSIONATA

What was Beethoven's appearance in his 'thirties?

The powerful torso was still held erect by the short legs. The slightly pock-marked face was now becoming deeply lined. The angles of the jaw and the protrudding lower lip were becoming more prominent. The nose, aptly described in these years as "four-square like a lion's," was flatter. The little smouldering eyes (no one agrees what color they were) impressed every observer; in some moods they could be frightening. Beethoven's teeth were perfect throughout his life. His hair had not yet turned gray, but it was becoming unruly. He had to shave up to his eyes and this operation generally left his face cut. His dress was more careless than before, and his deportment—naturally, since his absorption in his thoughts was greatly increased by his deafness—more eccentric. Earlier he had acquired a habit of pacing his rooms while composing and spitting from the window; now he would sometimes absentmindedly spit in the mirror. Ignatz von Seyfried, a contemporary conductor, describes Beethoven's lodgings at this time:

> Books and music were scattered in every corner; here the remnants of a cold luncheon; here sealed or half-emptied bottles; here upon a stand the hurried sketches of a quartet; here the remains of a *dejeuner*; there on the pianoforte on scribbled paper, the material for a glorious symphony still slumbering in embryo; here a proof sheet awaiting salvation; friendly and business letters covering the floor; between the windows a respectable loaf of strachino, *ad latus* a considerable ruin of a genuine Veronese salami.

Young Ries confirms the description:

> Beethoven was very clumsy and awkward in his movements; his gestures were totally lacking in grace. He seldom took up anything without dropping it and breaking it. Thus he repeatedly threw his inkwell into the piano that stood next to his writing desk. No piece of furniture was safe, least of all a valuable one; everything was knocked over, dirtied and destroyed. It is difficult to understand how he succeeded in shaving himself even without taking into account the frequent cuts on his cheeks. He could never learn to dance in time.

Once, in the summer of 1804, Ries went for a very long walk with Beethoven in the country near Döbling:

> He had been all the time humming and sometimes howling, always up and down, without singing any definite notes. In answer to my question what it was, he said: "A theme for the last movement of the Sonata has occurred to me." When we entered the room he ran to the pianoforte without taking off his hat. I took a seat in a corner and he soon forgot all about me. Now he stormed for at least an hour with the beautiful finale of the Sonata. Finally he got up, was surprised still to see me, and said: "I can't give you a lesson today, I must do some more work."

This was the "Appassionata," a piano epic so overpowering in its dynamics that it was not to be played publicly for a decade after Beethoven's death, and so broad in its implications that Romain Rolland was not to deal adequately with it in sixty-seven pages. Liszt, who described the little *Allegretto* of the "Moonlight" as *"une fleure entre deux abêmes,"* would better have thus described the *Andante con moto* of the "Appassionata," except that the short set of variations could only be likened to the life-cycle of some transcendental experience. The abrupt transition from the two first movements to the Finale which Ries was lucky enough to hear first, and which consists of two arpeggiated chords, *pianissimo* and *fortissimo,* followed by thirteen reverberating staccatos, may well be the most dramatic moment in the literature of the keyboard. *Attacca l'Allegro!* Beethoven wrote under it, and he who does not truly attack what follows had better devote his efforts henceforth to less titanic fare.

58

"Here," writes Burk, "and in the 'Waldstein' Sonata of the next year [he must mean "last"] there was a sweeping impetuosity as if the lover's sighs of Jean Paul's Titan or Goethe's Werther had suddenly become as overwhelming and convincing as their authors would have liked to make them. He had overflowed his mold, as with the *Eroica* Symphony he had strained the limits of the chamber orchestra of the time, and fairly burst the four elegant walls of Lichnowsky's princely salon, where that music was first tried . . . [so now] the new sonatas, if played according to their plain implications, would have threatened wreckage upon the instruments of the time."

In that same summer the lyrical G Major Piano Concerto, the three epoch-making quartets for Count Rasoumovsky, and that flawless embodiment of buoyant affirmation, the Fourth Symphony, were all started; and they were finished before the year's close.

FIDELIO

Beethoven must have been working on his opera *Fidelio,* too, for he had begun composing it the year before, and it was to be performed for the first time the year after, 1806.

Why did Beethoven write an opera at all? He was equipped for it neither by training nor musical inclination. Ambition must be the answer, for by this route alone lesser composers—Paer, Cherubini, Vogler, Seyfried, Salieri—were achieving more recognition and richer rewards. Beethoven admired Cherubini rather extravagantly; but for the others—how could he possibly fail, where such midgets had succeeded? Another motive must be considered. Throughout his career Beethoven toyed with the idea of communicating more explicitly than "abstract" sounds would permit, the content of his emotional response to life. The funeral march in the A-flat piano sonata, parts of the *Pastoral* Symphony, and a number of compositions still to come, are frankly programmatic. It was a mistake, but an understandable one. Nor would the "pure" music be so movingly "impure" in all its deeper meanings were the composer less concerned to share all that he feels. "To put the matter in unfashionable terms," Tovey remarks, "Beethoven's music is edifying. There is nothing inartistic in that. . . . Beethoven's sense of duty was to preach."

60

The already shopworn libretto of *Fidelio,* with its sentimental plot and improbable psychology, nevertheless provided Beethoven with an ideal preachment. Leonora's sacrificial love for Florestan the prisoner of tyranny, though ostensibly set in Spain, was in its origins an episode of the French Revolution. Better still, it was a true story of the Terror. In other words, Beethoven may have thought to himself as he read it, revolutions *per se* settle nothing. This he had already lived to see. As long as one individual is unjustly oppressed—in this case most appositely by the Revolution itself—one must go on struggling for justice.

With what weapons? With love, of course, and courage, and will. Why Florestan was imprisoned in the first place we are never told; and how his tormentor loses power is almost as mysterious. Emotionally, philosophically, musically, these details do not matter. Beethoven begins conventionally enough with a Mozartean duet. Once Leonora appears on the stage, however, any further pretense of concession to the public taste of the day is abandoned. Beethoven had found his ideal woman—the devoted self-sacrificing wife—just as in the *Eroica* he had described his ideal hero. Act One rises to ecstatic heights in Leonora's recognition of her task after overhearing that Pizarro intends to murder her husband. Her thoughts are given graver expression in the dialogue and Chorus of prisoners (*O Freiheit, kehrest du zurück . . .*) Suspense and dramatic intensity mount with Leonora's anxiety as the jailers close in on her loved one. An eerie groundswell of triplets in the strings perhaps suggested to Schubert his exciting accompaniment for the *Erlkönig.* But all of this is only preparation for the glorious music of Act II. Florestan appears for the first time, chained to the wall.

O grauenvolle Stille!

Süsser Trost in meinem Herzen:
Meine Pflicht hab ich getan.

In des Lebens Frülingstagen
Ist das Glück von mir gefloh'n

[*How horrible is the silence!*

My heart is only consoled by the trust
That I have done my duty.

In the springtime of life
Happiness fled from me.]

But his soliloquy rises to heights of beatific joy with the lines:

> *Im rosigen Duft sich tröstend zur*
> > *Seite mir stellet,*
> *Ein Engel, Leonoren, der Gattin so gleich*
> *Der führt mich zur Freiheit ins*
> > *himmlische Reich.*

> [*With words of comfort she restores me,*
> > *That angel, Leonora,*
> *Leading me to freedom and the heavenly*
> > *kingdom.*]

There follows a spoken dialogue between the jailor and Leonora (disguised as "Fidelio") outside the donjon, followed by another duet with macabre, Schubertian murmurings. The recognition, after prolonged delays, takes place when Pizarro enters to kill Florestan and Leonora throws herself between them. The rescue is effected and the lovers join in a soaring ensemble:

> *O namenlose Freude!*
> [*O inexpressible joy!*]

I have included these quotations to emphasize the seemingly autobiographical suggestions in the libretto which obviously appealed to Beethoven. Where they did not occur, he interpolated them. But the resulting musical fusion is not autobiographical; it is universal. The second could not come about without the first. For what can an artist truly express that he hasn't experienced? And what experience, unrelated to the general human condition, has any meaning but to mortal dust? Beethoven, like Florestan, had been imprisoned in the darkest of donjons—his deafness. He had loved. He had overcome fear. He had rediscovered joy—in his music. It is all here.

It would be foolish to assume that because Beethoven was not temperamentally disposed to writing operas, he produced a work of questionable value. *Fidelio* is a "failure" only in terms of Beethoven's instrumental successes. Among the masterpieces of opera from *Orfeo* and *Die Zauberflöte* to *Tristan* and *Otello* and *Wozzeck*, it holds its own; and there will always be some who prefer its dark, impassioned sincerity to any of them.

The vicissitudes of the actual writing of *Fidelio* read like some legend of a benign minotaur in a labyrinth. The difficulties Beethoven experienced with the writing—there are sketches for eighteen different beginnings to Florestan's great aria—were as nothing compared with the problems involved in its production. The descent of the French armies on Austria in 1805 coincided with the announcement of the first performance. Ulm fell on October 20, and Beethoven's old friend Bernadotte occupied Salzburg. Most of the potential audience fled the capital, and so did the principal singers. The parts fell to virtual amateurs. One week before the opening Vienna itself was occupied. Wounded soldiers were being brought into the city on stretchers from the Russian front to the East. Napoleon was in Schönbrunn Palace. As the curtain rose on the night of November 20, an audience of French officers applauded lightly this grim parable in an alien tongue. After three performances it folded.

One month later, after some stormy sessions with the management, the assembled musical personages of the city, and his friends, Beethoven agreed to cut the opera from three acts to two. Stephan von Breuning condensed the text. Beethoven enriched the score and wrote the second of four overtures, the one now known as "Leonora No. 3." A critic at the reopening referred to this greatest of overtures as "abominable cacophony." One further performance took place and *Fidelio* folded again.

A disastrous third-season revival was enlivened by a conversation between Beethoven and Baron Braun, owner of the opera house. Beethoven thought the Baron was cheating him of his proper share of the box-office and the Baron tried to mollify him by suggesting that more cheap seats could be put on sale:

BEETHOVEN: I don't write for the galleries.
BRAUN: My dear sir, even Mozart did not disdain to write for the galleries.
BEETHOVEN: (*shouting*) My score! Immediately!
              There will be no more performances!
              (*He stomps out with it*).

Seven years later, in 1814, Beethoven made his second complete revision of *Fidelio* with the very practical help of Treitschke. This poet has left a vivid description of one episode of their collaboration, his re-writing of Florestan's aria:

What I am now relating will remain always in my memory. He read it, ran up and down the room, muttered, growled, as was his habit instead of singing—and tore open the pianoforte. My wife had often begged him to play; today he placed the text in front of him and began to improvise marvelously—music which no magic could hold fast. Out of it he seemed to conjure the motive of the aria. The hours went by, but Beethoven improvised on. Supper, which he had intended to eat with us, was served, but—he would not be disturbed. It was late when he embraced me, and declining the meal hurried home. The next day the admirable composition was finished!

This time the opera was well received. Six performances followed. The last, out of season and for the benefit of the composer, was a sellout. At the bottom of a piano transcription Beethoven wrote grimly under the words, "fine, with God's help": *O man, help yourself.*

The rest of his life Beethoven was to search vainly for another suitable libretto. He considered the plays of Schiller and Voltaire; he weighed *Faust* and *Macbeth* and *Romeo and Juliet;* he pondered classical subjects galore. He conferred with all the available poets of the time. But he never found what he was looking for. "I care little what genre the work belongs to, so the material be attractive to me," he told Rellstab, "but it must be something which I can take up with sincerity and love. I would not compose operas like *Don Juan* and *Figaro.* They are repugnant to me. I could not choose such subjects. They are too frivolous." This moral horror of Mozart's dramatic versatility is described by Shaw as puritanism—"The Puritan who is in every Sansculotte"—but Beethoven, no Shavian, knew what he was doing. Once, when offered a fairy subject, *Bradamante,* he remarked: "As to magic, I cannot deny that I am prejudiced against that sort of thing because it so often demands that both emotion and intellect shall be put to sleep." We should be grateful that *Fidelio* gave Beethoven the opportunity to exercise both.

THE "IMMORTAL BELOVED"

Was Beethoven's search for the ideal woman "sublimated," as we now glibly put it, in his musical description of the devoted, self-sacrificing Leonore? Not at all. Musically he had made his choice, at least for the time being. In life, he kept right on looking. "When we walked past a rather attractive girl," Ries reports, "he would turn around, look at her again sharply through his glasses, and laugh or grin when he found I observed him." But Beethoven, normal in this as in all impulses, wanted also to possess and be possessed. And the record of the desperate search, for which he was thoughtless enough to provide few clues, has kept literary detectives busy for a century.

64

Therese von Brunswick, Barbara Keglevics, Josephine Deym, Giulietta Guiccardi, Marie von Erdödy, Theresa Malfatti, Magdalena Willmann, Amalie Sebald,
Rahel Levin, all beautiful and desirable, pass through Beethoven's life in these
years. For most of them he felt at least very strong attraction, and several are
known to have felt as much for him.

The search has generally centered on the identity of the "Immortal Beloved"
to whom Beethoven addressed a celebrated letter. This letter, bearing no names or
addresses and a baffling confusion of dates, was found in a secret drawer of Beethoven's desk shortly after the composer's death. With it was the Heiligenstadt Testament, two miniatures, and the bankshares the searchers were looking for. Who was
the lady to whom the letter was addressed? Researchers—most recently the late
Dana Steichen in an enormous tome that is convincing on almost every aspect of
Beethoven except the mystery it purports to solve—each has a candidate. The
mystery will never be solved. And if it could be, it wouldn't matter. What does
matter is the evidence that Beethoven was in love with many women during these
years of his prime and that some of his recorded thoughts on these experiences have
a bearing on his music. To consider the evidence on this subject contained in the
celebrated letter, we will rely on Mrs. Steichen's translation, presumably her own:

The 6th July   *Morning.—*

My angel, my all, my self.—only a few words to day and of course with pencil (with
yours)—not till tomorrow will my lodgings be definitely determined upon—what an unworthy waste of time for such things—why this deep grief where necessity speaks—can our
love exist except through sacrifices, except through not demanding everything, can you
change it that you are not wholly mine, I not wholly thine—O God look at beautiful Nature
and calm your mind about what must be—Love demands everything and rightly, so it is
to me with you, you with me—only you forget so easily, that I must live *for me* and *for you*,
were we wholly united, you would feel the pain of it as little as I—My journey was terrible,
I did not arrive here until 4 o'clock yesterday morning, lacking horses the post-chaise chose
another route, but what a terrible one, at the station before the last I was warned not to
travel at night, made fearful of a forest, but that only made me the more eager and I was
wrong; the coach must needs break down on the terrible road, a bottomless mere country
road—without such postilions as I had with me, I should have stuck on the way. Esterhazy
traveling the usual road hitherward, had the same fate with eight horses as I had with four.
—yet I got some pleasure out of it, as I always do when I happily overcome something—
now quickly from outer things to the inner,—we shall soon, I suppose, see each other; even

66

today I cannot communicate to you the observations I have made during the last few days about my life—if our hearts were always close together I would make none of the kind. My heart is full of many things to say to you—Ah—there are moments when I find that speech is nothing at all—cheer up—remain my true my only treasure, my all, as I am yours, the gods must send us the rest, what for us must be and shall be.—

Your faithful
Ludwig—

Evening Monday the 6th July—

You are suffering you my most precious being—only now have I learned that letters must be posted very early in the morning, Mondays—Thursdays—the only days on which the mail-coach goes from here to K. —You are suffering—Ah, where I am, you are also with me, with me and you I will manage so that I can live with you, what a life!!!! so!!!! without you—pursued by the goodness of mankind here and there, which I as little wish to deserve as I deserve it—Humility of man toward man—it pains me—and when I consider myself in connection with the universe, what am I and what is he whom we call the Greatest—and yet—again herein is the godliness of man—I weep when I think that you will probably not receive the first message from me until Saturday evening—much as you love me—I love you more—never hide from me anything that is you—good night—as I am taking the baths I must go to sleep—[*two long words crossed out*] O God— so near! so far! is it not truly a celestial edifice our love—but also as firm as the vaults of heaven.—

Good morning on 7th July—

Though still in bed my thoughts go out to you my immortal beloved, here and there joyfully then again sadly, waiting to learn whether or not Fate will hear us—I can live only wholly with you or not at all, yes I am resolved to wander far away until I can fly to your arms and say that I am really at home, send my soul enwrapped in you into the land of spirits—yes unhappily it must be—you will compose your mind all the more since you know my fidelity to you, never can another possess my heart, never—never—O God why must one part from what one so loves, and yet my life in V. is as now a miserable life— your love makes me the happiest and the unhappiest of men at the same time—at my age now I require a uniform sameness of life—can this be under our relations?—Angel, I have just learned that the mail-coach goes every day—therefore I must close at once so that you may receive the l. [letter] at once—Be calm, only by calm contemplation of our existence can we reach our goal to live together—be calm—love me—today—yesterday—what yearning with tears for you—you—Oh love me on and on—never misjudge the most faithful heart of your beloved

L.
forever thine
forever mine
forever us

I don't think I have ever seen this poignant outpouring commented on in any but the (irrelevant) terms of to whom it could have been addressed. Parallels with the music suggest themselves in almost every phrase, but to pursue them systematically would be pointless. I will confine myself to isolating what seems most obviously related to Beethoven's art in this letter which was either never posted, or returned to Beethoven after a quarrel. Consider these phrases:

(1) why this deep grief where necessity speaks—
 can our love exist except through sacrifices
(2) Love demands everything and rightly
(3) I got some pleasure out of it (the coach's breakdown) as I always do when I happily overcome something
(4) the gods must send us the rest, what for us must be and shall be.—
(5) when I consider myself in connection with the universe, what am I and what is he whom we call the Greatest—and yet—again herein is the godliness of man. . . .
(6) my thoughts go out to you [other translators have it "surge toward you"] my immortal beloved, here and there joyfully and again sadly, waiting to learn whether or not Fate will hear us
(7) you know my fidelity
(8) your love makes me the happiest and unhappiest of men at the same time
(9) Be calm, only by calm contemplation of our existence

(3) and (7) bespeak characteristics already alluded to, Beethoven's will and his loyalty: the will revealed in the decade of struggle over *Fidelio*; the loyalty given voice through Leonora, so gratefully acknowledged by friends, soon to be so bitterly resented by his nephew.

(6) recalls the polarities of the music of the Second Period, surging as it does "here and there joyfully and again sadly," but still generating in this conflict such discord, aggression and war as the Fifth Symphony and the "Emperor" Concerto make manifest; while (8) suggests the synthesis first attempted in the "Rasoumovsky" Quartets.

(1) and (9) look forward to the philosophic tenets that fortified Beethoven in his final years—the doctrine of Necessity here anticipated in his acceptance of whatever doomed this love. It is characteristic of Beethoven to prefer "sacrifice" to expedients. "Sensual enjoyment," he was to write in his Notebooks later on, "without the union of souls is and always will be bestial: after it, there is no trace of an exalted sentiment, rather one feels remorse." It is also characteristic of Beethoven that he didn't assume any such thing; obviously he had experimented with promis-

cuous affairs and gone on to something that satisfied more.

(4) and (5) also foreshadow the Third Period, with the emphasis on religion. (5) shows Beethoven not to have made up his mind yet whether man had not better help himself unassisted. I may be wrong, but I believe this is the last time Beethoven refers to "the gods." In his early writings he almost invariably uses the plural. (4), however, looks forward to an ultimate acceptance of fate as embodied in the phrase recurring throughout his letters: *es muss sein.* Beethoven had a long way to travel, though, "from outer things to the inner" as he puts it here, before such fatalism could become uniformly affirmative.

(2) requires no comment, being the embodiment of the man and his music.

One question persists, the matter of "sublimation." Paul Henry Lang raises it in a discussion of Handel's enigmatic love life: "Complete devotion, the complete sharing of sentiments which is what love means, is more difficult for the creative artist than for anyone else. The more profound his devotion to his art, the less he can be sacrificed, and he fears the loss of his identity by being dissolved in another." Had Beethoven come to feel any such thing consciously, the ardent love poetry that is articulated in his work would have subsided to a stammer. Only toward the very end of his life when he perceived everything (without, we are tempted to say, understanding anything) does Beethoven come close to admitting this truth to himself. Had any hope of a conjugal life remained, he could not have conceived the thought. "If I had wished," he told Schindler in 1823, "to give my vital powers with that life [marriage], what would have remained for what is better, nobler?"

PATRONS AND PUBLISHERS

All during the decade of Beethoven's maturity and fame, he had as a pupil, in both piano playing and composition, the Emperor's brother. Rudolph of Habsburg was not a brilliant performer and he certainly had no talent for writing music. Yet Czerny says that the irascible Beethoven was always patient with him. Year after year he would correct the dull exercises and when the Archduke on occasion did come up with a finished piece Beethoven would congratulate him handsomely. All Beethoven's letters to the Archduke are of course deferential. He was not obliged to go further than this. If he had exhibited the touch of arrogance he generally affected when he chose to remind the nobility who was master, his conduct would have been tolerated. Once, for instance, when the Empress asked him to call upon her he sent back word that he was too busy. But for Rudolph—though he once remarked to a friend that he had one pupil left which was one too many—Beethoven seems to have felt affection. He dedicated to him from this period the exquisite *Lebewohl* Sonata, the G Major and E-flat ("Emperor") Concertos, the B-flat ("Archduke") Trio, and the second of the two violin sonatas in G Major, the piano part of which the Archduke was the first to play. From the last period, Rudolph received the dedications to the *Hammerklavier* Sonata (Opus 106) and the one in C Minor (Beethoven's last), the *Missa Solemnis,* and the posthumously published *Grosse Fugue.*

What had the Archduke done to deserve this king's ransom in immortal honors? He had done a great deal. In 1809 Beethoven was thinking seriously of leaving Vienna. War had come to the capital—"a destructive savage life is raging all around me! Nothing but drums, cannons, human misery of every kind." At times he had to muffle his head in pillows to protect the remnants of his hearing. "The whole course of events," he wrote his publishers, "has affected me physically and spiritually." Now Beethoven was at the height of his powers—let anyone who doubts it listen to the A Major Cello Sonata of that year—and had no intention of being buffeted by the winds of chance. He was about to accept an offer to be a musical figurehead at the court of Jerome Buonaparte, the new King of Westphalia, when Countess Erdödy, at whose home he had been living and to whom he had just dedicated the two magnificent Trios of Opus 70, heard about it. She prevailed on the Archduke to enlist the aid of two of his princely associates, and the three of them promptly offered Beethoven a yearly annuity of 4,000 florins for as long as he would remain in the capital.

Beethoven accepted. But his business troubles were only beginning. First Prince Lobkowitz went bankrupt, then Prince Kinsky was thrown from a horse; that left the Archduke his sole guarantor. (With the inflation of the currency, the doubling of his expenses, and the steadily increasing unpopularity of his new music, Beethoven really needed that annuity.) In an effort to recoup the lost two-thirds of his grant, he went to the courts. And now it was that the more Beethoven found himself in an outside world whose values and rewards were quantitative, the more he

70

withdrew into an inner one of his own, tied to the other by no more than a fantasy of persecution. Friends became potential traitors, publishers "hellhounds who lick and gnaw at my brains." The fickle public was brazenly, as he saw it, entertaining the harlot of Italian opera.

We are now on the threshold of that misty mid-kingdom, Beethoven's business ethics. The first investigation into it shocked the righteous Thayer a hundred years ago. Thayer's shock in turn led Sullivan to propound the theory of a Beethoven whose business morality must be considered noble "though not identical with business morality." The more common-sensical Burk could not agree with this and observes with considerable justice that "What Beethoven failed to understand was that society was not so constituted as to give him an unassailable niche and entire artistic freedom. His patrons and his publishers were, no less than he, subject to misfortune, and this truth he never learned to accept."

In one respect, at least, Beethoven was very far ahead of his time—and ours. He saw that the artist, unless guaranteed some regular means of support, is going to have to soil his hands and waste his time in the market place. "It is not my final purpose," he wrote his publishers, "as you believe, to become a musical usurer in art, who writes only to enrich himself. God forbid! Yet I am fond of an independent life; this I cannot lead without a little wealth and, besides, even his fee must yield an artist some honor, even as honor must surround everything that he undertakes." He seems to have done some thinking on the practical problem involved. "There should be only a single Art Exchange in the world," he wrote another publisher. "The artist could simply send his works there, to be given as much as he needs; as it is, one has to be half a merchant on top of everything else, and how badly one goes about it!"

Beethoven's offer of the Mass in D to five different publishers simultaneously, if they would guarantee to publish his complete works, is generally cited as the worst example of "how badly" he went about it; but there is some evidence that the publishers themselves were already dangling the half-promise to bring out a complete works as a means of getting exclusive rights to the Mass. As far as the public is concerned, the burden of proof is always on the artist; it is assumed that publishers are "practical" and honest, artists "impractical" and at best amoral. The artist is expected to be selffless. Beethoven, who was emancipating the musician

at the same time that he was emancipating music, would have accomplished nothing in the first instance had he gone about it in a gentlemanly way. Societies based on force respect only forceful people. When Beethoven felt himself insulted at a dinner, he didn't merely leave, he first upset the table. Those who wanted good music, his at any rate, would pay well for it. "Beethoven," an observant acquaintance remarked, "seems very interested in money and I must confess that this makes him more human."

He was interested in money for the practical reasons already cited. If he became a sharp bargainer, and toward the end something of a miser, there is no reason to suppose that this lapse in any way affected his art. Beethoven who solved all his problems in art solved very few in life. He recognized the paradox. "A man," he wrote Goethe's musical advisor, Zelter, "is often impelled on his own account, or on account of others, so he must lower himself, yet even this is part of human destiny."

GOETHE FACE TO FACE

Goethe himself was incapable of understanding Beethoven and this turned out to be one of the composer's bitterest disappointments. When a newspaper critic once asked Beethoven how he happened to quote the poet Klopstock, he answered: "You smile that I should have read Klopstock! I gave myself up to him many years —when I took my walks and at other times. Ah well! I did not always understand him. He is so restless; and he always begins too far away, from on high down; always *Maestoso* D-flat major. . . . Why should he always want to die? That will come soon enough. . . . But Goethe—he lives and wants us all to live with him."

It is possible that had Beethoven been confronted in his prime by a composer of his own dimensions, he would have found the experience disturbing. Certainly Michelangelo treated his only living intellectual and artistic rival with furious antagonism. But Goethe, as a writer, was no threat to Beethoven, as Leonardo had seemed to Michelangelo. From the moment of first reading his poems, the composer yearned to exchange "thoughts" on the highest level with the one European who was clearly of his stature. The opportunity arose most unexpectedly.

In the spring of 1810 Beethoven had been working on incidental music to Goethe's *Egmont.* Seated at the piano one day, he felt hands on his shoulders. He

turned and saw a young girl whose beauty and fame were known to everyone—
Bettina Brentano. This intellectual siren of Romanticism had three years ago thrown
herself into the arms of the fifty-eight-year-old Goethe and gone on to have a memo-
rable correspondence with him. Now, it seems, Bettina had heard the "Moonlight"
Sonata and made up her mind to effect a more difficult conquest. Beethoven
was only forty but he was notoriously unfriendly to celebrity hunters, though he
had never encountered a collector of geniuses. As it turned out, there was no difficulty at all. The composer gallantly said, "I have just written a beautiful song for
you. Do you want to hear it?" And, according to Bettina, he then sang in his incredible deaf-man's voice, yet movingly, his setting of Goethe's *Kennst du das Land*.

Other songs by Goethe followed. There were many meetings, and long talks
which, because of Bettina's propensity to dramatize her philosophy-inducing

74

charms, even on occasion at the cost of forging letters, are not always to be trusted. It is a fact, nevertheless, that because Bettina was quite alone in her time in recognizing the future's interest in Beethoven's ideas, she alone asked him the questions we would ask today. We are dependent upon her, consequently, for much that is unavailable elsewhere. "At least," Romain Rolland said, "she did not depart from the spirit of the truth."

Part of Bettina's ambition, of course, was to bring the two great men together. The meeting finally took place in the summer of 1812 at Teplitz, a fashionable watering-place in Bohemia. Beethoven, characteristically, was keyed up. "I would have gone to my death for him then, yes ten times over," he was to remark later. Goethe was characteristically reserved. Perhaps their encounter was doomed from the start. Bettina's relationship with the poet, who had many other beauties to flatter him, was deteriorating. Goethe's long-suffering wife had slapped her down, and Goethe himself was irritated by her scorn for "that Philistine" Zelter who regarded Beethoven's music as "immoral" and even "perverted." At first Goethe had been impressed. "Never before," he wrote his wife in Weimar, "have I seen an artist with more power of concentration, more energy, more inwardness." But as Beethoven improvised furiously, Goethe began to sense something alien to his circumspect, gentlemanly ways. His response—"Charming!"—could hardly have been what Beethoven anticipated. Goethe was still a man of the eighteenth century. Beethoven was this himself only in a sense Goethe was not musically equipped to appreciate—in the music's formal substructure, and in the tremendous *control* exercised over even the most emotional of passages. But in his life, as in the content of his music, Beethoven was all nineteenth century—from appearance and dress to lodgings and manner of speech. "If you don't recognize me as your equal," Beethoven complained bluntly to Goethe, "who will? To what beggarly mob must I play to find understanding?" Goethe may have sensed, too, a passion in the music, even an imaginative and architectonic capacity beyond anything in the philosophizings of *Faust.*

The well-known story of Goethe at the garden party, bowing deferentially to the Emperor while Beethoven lowers his hat and strides grimly across the path of the royal party is almost certainly Bettina's fabrication. It doesn't ring true to Beethoven's character to have said, "Let us walk on, arm and arm. They will have to get out of our way, not we out of theirs!" Ten years earlier, perhaps; in 1812 Beethoven's social position was secure. But Beethoven did write his publishers, "Goethe is too fond of the Court atmosphere, far fonder than is compatible with the dignity of a poet." And Goethe did write priggishly to Zelter: "Beethoven's . . . talent amazes me but, unfortunately, he has no self-control whatever. He is no doubt right in finding the world detestable, but by behaving as he does he really does not make it any more pleasant for himself or for others."

Years later Beethoven made one more effort. His admiration for Goethe's poetry never wavered. He had continued setting the songs and dedicating them to the poet. But at the time of the writing of the Mass in D, Beethoven had written Goethe a long letter, asking him if he would intercede ("I have written so much, but earned so little") with the Grand Duke of Weimar for a subscription. "A few words from you," he concluded, "would envelope me in bliss." Goethe not only failed to mention this small matter to his patron; he didn't bother to answer Beethoven's letter.

HUMOR—AND SHAKESPEARE

Most of the big works of Beethoven's second period have been mentioned, at least in passing. How to characterize this music as a whole? Three qualities may be artificially isolated: *humor*; a driving, sustained *energy*; and the first intimations of that *synthetic treatment* of joy and suffering that characterizes the music of the Third Period.

The humor in Beethoven's music is a quality he shares as abundantly with no other tragic artist in any of the arts but Shakespeare. Brueghel, Rembrandt and Handel come close. There is no humor in Michelangelo or Titian, Sophocles or Milton. We think of Cervantes, Molière, Rabelais, as essentially comic masters. What Mozart and Haydn had was *wit*, and a great sense of fun, and of some intermediate emotion—poised, in a way we hardly comprehend, between laughter and tears. Brahms' humor (like Goethe's) is a little labored; the spectacle of the *Herr Doktor* undertaking to be light is more likely to make one laugh at him than with him. In Beethoven, as in Shakespeare, the humor breaks out when the burden of anguish becomes unbearable, and in both cases it comes from the belly not the head.

Both artists are full of a different kind of merriment in their youth. The scenes with Mercutio and the Nurse in *Romeo and Juliet* may be compared with the first group of Bagatelles (Opus 33) and the Minuet and Rondo that follow the tragic Largo of the D Major Sonata. Further along, *As You Like It* and the *Pastoral* Symphony, with its country dances, thunder showers, and birdcalls, are a perfect parallel.

But the resemblance goes deeper, having to do not so much with the nature of art as with its purpose. What is art for? It is to heal men's souls by a revelation. But this revelation can never be convincing if it conceals or denies the pain over which it triumphs. Rising courageously above the misery that is most men's lot, its intoxicating message of beauty, humor, joy, is a moral proposition demanding creative participation to be effective therapy. Beethoven's most extensive testimony

is quoted by Bettina in a letter to Goethe:

> When I open my eyes I must sigh, for what I look upon is contrary to my religion, and I must despise the world which never divines that music is a greater revelation than the whole of wisdom and philosophy; music is the wine that incites us to new creation and I am the Bacchus who presses this glorious wine for mankind and grants them drunkenness of spirit; when they are sober again they will have fished up much which they may take with them on to dry land. . . . nor am I at all anxious about the fate of my music; its fate cannot be other than happy; whoever succeeds in grasping it shall be absolved from all the misery that bows down other men.

Shakespeare's testimony is in his plays, which may be interpreted similarly; but he was quite explicit about tone-poetry at least once:

> *Preposterous ass! That never read so far*
> *To know the cause why music was ordain'd!*
> *Was it not to refresh the mind of man*
> *After his studies or his usual pain?*

For psychological equivalents to the grave scene in *Hamlet,* or the Fool and mock-madman in *King Lear,* one must go to the Scherzos of the Fifth and Ninth Symphonies. Even in Beethoven's bantering letters, especially those to Zmeskall and Gleichenstein, there is a ring of the true Shakespearean laugh. One hears it when he addresses the self-important Schindler "Master flash-in-the-pan, and wide-of-the-mark! Full of reasons, yet devoid of reason!" or asks his publisher to find him a Mass by Bach "in which occurs a Basso ostinato resembling yourself" or chides the slothful proof-reader: "Mistakes—mistakes—you yourself are a unique mistake."

To analyze humor in music is as killing to its essence as to explain a joke. Tovey gives a try in the following comment on the second "Rasoumovsky" quartet:

"The finale . . . placed in circumstances where every listener will expect it to be in E Minor, insists on making the very same point by obstinately beginning in C Major and returning to that key again and again from its proper E Minor with a jerk as vicious as that of of any carter pulling his cart out of a rut."

Another kind of humor expresses itself in Beethoven through syncopation, of which there is every variety, from the delicate variations of the G Major Sonata of Opus 14, through the irresistibly propulsive finale of the E-flat Sonata of Opus 27, to the spreadeagled diabolism of the six Bagatelles (Opus 126) and the ethereal leaps of the last quartet. "Greenhorns," Shaw says, "write of syncopation now as if it were a new way of giving the utmost impetus to a musical measure, but the rowdiest jazz sounds like The Maiden's Prayer after Beethoven's Third Leonora Overture; and certainly no Negro corrobery that I ever heard could inspire the blackest dancer with such *diable au corps* as the last movement of the Seventh Symphony."

Lang sees another kind of humor in the pseudo-minuet of the Eighth. A satire on Biedermeier docility he calls it:

> Everything goes wrong in this movement: it has difficulty in getting started with its overemphasized and heavy-footed tentative lines; then the horns, trumpets, and tympani, missing their cue, hurl their ponderous tones at the wrong places and get entangled in the cadence. The finale, one of the longest Beethovenian movements, romps about with unrestricted merriment. Suddenly, in the midst of the swift but subdued flow in C major, the full orchestra crashes in with a resounding C sharp and pandemonium follows. The Homeric laughter ceases and the composer gives us immediately a calming and ingratiating melody, but only to soothe us, for there is an endless store of surprises waiting for the listener.

Still another and gentler sort of good spirits is in the frolicsome ripple of such *perpetuum mobile* movements as the Allegretto to the F Major Sonata of 1804 which I believe to be the ancestor of every Scherzo and Etude by Chopin; and the somewhat similar but more sublimely pearling rhythms of Therese von Brunswick's little F-sharp Sonata of 1809.

THE LIMITS OF SENSUOUS EXPERIENCE

Energy is much harder to define as a prevailing characteristic of the "Middle" Beethoven, but no one familiar with this music can fail to be stirred by it. There is energy, of course, in early Beethoven, but it is spasmodic; the energy of the Second Period blows like a trade-wind off Hatteras, or the kind of gale-force that passes through one standing alone at night on the prow of a swift ship. Parry called the fifteen drum-punctured bars-of-nothing in the Fifth Symphony "infinitely more impressive than the greatest noise ever made by Meyerbeer." But the Seventh Symphony exhibits this kind of energy in its most sustained form. Wagner saw in it the apotheosis of the dance; and this is true if "dance" be interpreted broadly to mean all that is daemonic and even orgiastic. The Finale caused one commentator to swear Beethoven must have seen the sea. (He could have, but only as an 11-year-old on that trip to Holland with his mother, concerning which his only known

80

comment was: "The Dutch are skin-flints.") But the monolithic Seventh differs from the more dramatic Fifth in respect to the remaining quality we spoke of as distinguishing Beethoven's central phase. It points the way to the synthesized emotional expression to come. Who can say, for example, what emotion the grave Allegretto of the Seventh projects? Is its sombre yet buoyant march rhythm indicative of sorrow or joy? It includes both, and simultaneously. After Heiligenstadt Beethoven rarely expressed mere defiance: he no longer felt fear. "In the same way that you are now able to throw yourself into the whirlpool of society," he wrote in the margin of the third "Rasoumovsky" quartet, "so you are able to write your works in spite of all social hindrances. Let your deafness no longer be a secret —even for art."

Especially in the "Rasoumovsky" quartets did Beethoven manage for the first time to drop all his defenses. Now at last he could write so beyond limitations of class and education, so objectively in depth of feeling, that the profoundest thoughts seem to explain themselves and the simplest listener hears his own voice. "Show me the racecourse at whose distant end the palm tree stands!" he wrote in 1813, "Lend sublimity to my highest thoughts, enrich them with truths that remain truths forever!" Thus far—if we interpret this verbal "raptus" to define an art embracing the limits of sensuous experience—the music had answered his prayer.

Darkness
and
the
Illumined
Night

1814-1827

DIALOGUE—THE LAPSE

The scene is the garden of Imperial Ambassador Count Rasoumovsky's palace, adjoining the temporary wooden structure at the rear built to accommodate the hundreds of Congress of Vienna guests Czar Alexander is entertaining. The ball is over. The wooden structure has just caught fire. The guests in their formal attire are watching the efforts of dozens of servants and firemen vainly attempting to keep the flames from spreading to the palace proper. The host, moving from group to group in an effort to keep spirits up, approaches Beethoven who stands alone by a tree.

COUNT RASOUMOVSKY: (*jokingly*) Well, Beethoven, you of all my guests have least reason to look downcast. To be sure, the library will go next, with the manuscripts of our three quartets, but fortunately the scores are already published and music like that would survive in the memories of music-lovers even were all the libraries in the world to burn.

BEETHOVEN: With my commiseration to you for your losses, your Excellency, I was not thinking of your ashes, but mine.

RASOUMOVSKY: Your ashes? You've had a fire too?

BEETHOVEN: Always a fire. The trouble with mine is, it's gone out.

RASOUMOVSKY: How can you say that? Why, I attended the concert of your music in the *Redoutensaal* last week. I don't believe an audience anywhere ever applauded music louder or longer.

BEETHOVEN: And *what* were they applauding?

RASOUMOVSKY: The "Battle of Vittoria"—wildly; that cantata honoring our Congress, "The Glorious Moment"—almost as enthusiastically; and even the "companion piece" as they called it, your Sixth Symphony—

BEETHOVEN: Seventh. . . . It received no notice at all. And it was the only honest work on the program. The fools! I never pandered to the common taste—never till now.

RASOUMOVSKY:	Even Homer nodded now and then, they say.
BEETHOVEN:	I am not nodding. That's the worst of it. I'm burnt out. I write this balderdash for Mälzel because I have nothing further to say in a serious vein. And as for the "Glorious Moment," this victory over Napoleon the world's conservatives are celebrating, I wrote better when I believed in him, when the pyromaniac was still at large—
RASOUMOVSKY:	Rumor has it that he's at large again, that he's escaped from Elba and is on his way to Paris—
BEETHOVEN:	(*sourly*) Good. Perhaps he hasn't burnt enough of the world yet. Perhaps man won't change his ways until the fire has consumed every individual home and scorched every bad conscience. I include mine.

Everything referred to in this imagined conversation during the great fire of December 31, 1814, had happened or was happening to Beethoven. His curious friendship with Johann Nepomuk Mälzel, inventor of the metronome, had had one happy consequence and many distracting ones. The happy one had been the inspiration for the witty *Allegretto scherzando* of the Eighth Symphony, completed in 1812, with its wind instruments imitating the regular staccato beats of the ticking machine. The distracting consequences came the following year when Mälzel's propensity to turn his mechanical gadgets into gold happened to coincide with a momentary compulsion on Beethoven's part to get-rich-quick. The failure of Princes Lobkowitz and Kinsky to meet their two-thirds' obligation in the promised annuity had exacerbated Beethoven's existing sense of economic insecurity. Nanette Streicher, wife of a piano-maker Beethoven was friendly with at the time, had been concerned enough with the composer's disreputable living conditions to talk him into making some "sound investments." And since the years 1813-1815 were to witness Beethoven's greatest popularity during his lifetime, and therefore his peak income from royalties, it was already ordained that whatever prosperity might come to him should be "saved" for the objective in life toward which his thwarted capacity for love was already beginning to point.

Mälzel had bemused the Emperor Napoleon with an automatic chess-player. He now proceeded to bemuse Beethoven. First he constructed for him an "improved" ear-trumpet. Then in his workshop he revealed to the astonished composer his "improved" way of making music. This ingenious mechanical brass band, or "Panharmonicon" as he called it, was equipped with bellows controlled by a pin-studded revolving cylinder and it had already "played" Haydn's Military Symphony.

Its inventor now ventured to cash in on the enthusiasm for Wellington's victory over the Napoleonic armies in Spain—and what better way to do this than to have the world's foremost living composer write a "symphony" on the subject? Rationalizing his temporary musical depression with the thought that he was somehow contributing to the enlightened progress of science, Beethoven complied. The resulting atrocity is beautifully described by Marion Scott:

> Mozart could do one of his finest works—the Fantasia in F minor—for a musical clock, because his impulse was to compensate defects in others by his own inexhaustible wealth. But not so Beethoven. He knew the orchestration was inferior; with an almost childish delight he gave it music to match on a programme sketched by Mälzel. The opposing armies are represented by two groups of wind instruments: the remainder of the orchestra is as strongly "garrisoned" as possible. The tune *Rule Britannia* is the "motif" of the British; *Malbrouck* that of the French—a tune we know better under the name "We won't go home till morning"! When the battle is joined, copious cannon shots "enrich" the score, and after a Storm March, where the English drums make a most horrible din, *Malbrouck* wavers chromatically into a tremolo and dissolves. A triumphant march leads to *God Save the King*, treated first as a hymn of thanksgiving and later as the subject for a fugue. . . . Beethoven , like Haydn, had a warm admiration for this tune, but to English ears his fugue is almost ribald.

Miss Scott adds cogently that almost all Beethoven's works have some picture or "programme" as a starting-point, but that only in this one (as with such later composers as Richard Strauss) is the programme permitted to become the arriving-point. Put otherwise, Beethoven's content elsewhere unfolds in musical terms, here alone in pictorial-auditory symbols stripped of any inner emotional compulsion.

Beethoven was unhappy with this lapse almost as soon as he had committed it. He said he liked the "Battle" only "because it had thoroughly thrashed the Viennese." (Vienna was Beethoven's current scapegoat.) Instead of using the income from the composition's success to finance a tour of England, as he and Mälzel had planned, Beethoven invested his share and sat tight. The furious Mälzel tried to pirate the score for his own grand tour and Beethoven promptly sued him— the beginning of a series of legal actions that were to drag through the courts for years.

THE INFERTILE YEARS

The real motivation for Beethoven's lapse was not money but creative paralysis. He had said everything in his music that he had to say—or thought he had—and the confession of this is more poignantly conveyed by the years of infertility that were to follow than by the lapse. Premonition of this state of mind may be read into the anguished introduction to the last of the "Rasoumovsky" quartets, as far back as 1806, and more extensively into the F Minor Quartet of 1810 which Beethoven himself must have labelled *Serioso* in recognition of its unusual capitulation to brooding melancholy.

The four fallow years (1812-1816) are punctuated with all sorts of verbal clues to what was going on in Beethoven's mind. His alienation from Vienna and Viennese society has already been mentioned. Deafness had now virtually sealed off the social outlet to his emotions. "I can say with some truth," he wrote Amenda in 1815, "that I live almost alone in this, the largest city in Germany." Beethoven's obsessive dream of travel is about to begin. He looks longingly toward London. Inspired no doubt by Goethe, he talks of wandering through Italy "with a few artists." The letters are full of vague travel-talk. "Foreign countries will make you gentler, more human, more reconciled to the world," he tells his Notebook.

But in other moods, aware that there is no escape from his isolation by physical means, he feels his way gropingly toward some inner reconciliation:

Resignation [he confides to his diary of 1812], the most sincere resignation to your fate! Only this can make you capable of the sacrifices which your duty and vocation demand . . . make all the necessary arrangements for your distant journey . . . in spite of all, you must win through by defiance, be absolutely true to your constant conviction. . . . You must not be human, not for yourself, only for others: for you there can be no more happiness, except within yourself, in your art. O God! Give me strength to conquer myself! For nothing must bind me to this life. . . . O terrible circumstances that do not suppress my feeling for domesticity, but prevent its realization.

There is a reference here to a final effort to achieve happiness and fulfillment with a woman. How the effort was blasted is revealed in an exchange of letters with his friend Baron Gleichenstein two years before. Gleichenstein was engaged to Anna Malfatti, and Beethoven was hopelessly attracted to her eighteen-year-old sister, Therese. The ingenuous composer wrote Wegeler in Bonn for his birth-certificate but then his resolution seems to have wavered. Evidently anticipating a refusal he sent a letter of proposal to Gleichenstein and asked his friend to present it. The incredulous reaction of the light-hearted belle to this proposition on the part of her revered but "unattractive" music teacher may be imagined. The appalling wound to Beethoven's pride, if not his heart, is conveyed in the letter to Gleichenstein that followed the bad news:

> Your news hurled me from the regions of highest rapture to the lowest depths. Why add that you would let me know when there was to be music again? Am I then nothing more than a *musicus* to you and to the other? That seems at least to be the explanation. So, I can seek support only in my own breast; for me there is none from without. No, friendship and all kindred emotions have nothing but wounds for me. So be it then, for yourself, poor Beethoven, there is to be no happiness from without, you must create everything from within; only in the ideal world can you find friends.

"A TERRIBLE BEAUTY IS BORN"

The "philosophy" which Beethoven began to evolve from now on to cope with this and other frustrations may not be of great moment to philosophers. But, as a clue to the way in which he was able thus to solve his problems as an artist by making his art *continue in adversity* to express his noblest aspirations, it is of enduring interest. First comes the dim awareness that whatever solutions are possible must be fought out in the music itself:

> Submission, absolute submission to your fate. . . . You may no longer be a man, not for yourself, only for others. . . .

This passive phase of recognition, the phase that was to persist through the four unproductive years, is dated 1812. The first hint of a more active principle of reconciliation is contained in a letter of 1815. It is addressed to his great friend Countess Erdödy, herself a lifelong sufferer from physical ailments and domestic woes:

> We finite creatures with infinite spirits are born only to suffer and to rejoice, and one could almost say that only the most excellent . . . derive joy from suffering.

Countess Erdödy was a gifted amateur pianist and she surrounded herself with fine performers on the violin and cello; but we do not know to what extent such compositions as the two soul-searching cello sonatas (Opus 102) of 1815 dedicated to her served to alleviate her own sufferings. We do know, however, that in the following year a work of similar "philosophical" import grew directly out of Beethoven's concern to console a bereaved friend. I have already mentioned the pianist Dorothea Ertmann and Beethoven's "therapeutic" improvisation for her at his apartment in 1816, following the death of her last child. The sonata growing

out of this act of compassion, the A Major of Opus 101, constitutes the "break-through" (as we say today) from Beethoven's Second Period to his Third, a breakthrough in the light of what came after.

No dam broke—as yet. The A Major Sonata with its compressed style, its directions for expressiveness in German (*Geschwind, doch nicht zu sehr, und mit Entschlossenheit,* etc.), its abrupt changes of mood, its suggestions of unearthly joy, its tremendous fugal finale, point the way to the ultimate Beethoven. Yet in point of time this revolutionary work stands poised as though precipiced. Beethoven had the worst years of his life still to live; much time would have to pass before he could yield himself freely in his music to any such spirit of acceptance. The roiling travail of his next composition, the almost unbearable (and virtually unplayable) *Hammerklavier* Sonata, Opus 106, that was to occupy him for the two whole years of 1818-1819 speaks more tellingly in its air of frustrated giantism of the irresolution that had entered Beethoven's life. But before coming to the much-disputed cause of this last creative hiatus, let us look at the physical changes that had come over the composer as his contemporaries saw him in his last years.

DIRT AND DISORDER

From 1815 on, it becomes very difficult to cite any "objective" testimony on what Beethoven was like. As he entered his forty-fifth year he was technically "middle-aged" but any such phrase to describe him must impress the reader as ludicrous in the extreme; he was both far older and far younger than any of us at a like age will ever be. Close friends like Wegeler, Amenda, Stephan Bruening, Countess Erdödy, the Lichnowskys, were either far away or kept at a distance by the composer's increasing touchiness. Surrounded by factotums like Schindler, Oliva, and Holz, whose subservience he both scorned and depended upon, he tends in our eyes to become the creature of their alternating partisanship and recoil. Those who came from afar to visit him were for the most part hero-worshippers, awed by the Master's presence, reporting mainly what they had come to find. Thus the poet Rellstab, though disappointed not to find the "tempestuousness" of "wild genius" he had expected in the composer's features, found indeed "melancholy, suffering and kindness. . . . Not a single sign of hardness, nor of that great boldness which characterizes his spirit. . . . In spite of all this, he lost nothing of that mysterious attraction that draws us so powerfully and irresistibly to the exterior of great men." Rellstab found Beethoven's hair "grey, bushy and untidy," the face "much smaller than I had imagined," and the great man's complexion "brownish, but not that healthy and sturdy brown which the huntsman acquires, but mingled with a yellowish, sickly hue." Beethoven's nose, so lately described as "four-square like a lion's," has now become "narrow, sharp," and the once-insolent mouth, "benevolent."

Weber's son, Max, visiting Beethoven with his father about the same time, found "benevolence" in the "small, shining eyes beneath the bushy and sullenly contracted eyebrows" and testifies to the truth of "those marvelous dimples which all his portraits show, formed by two jawbones which seemed capable of cracking the hardest nuts." Beethoven was kind to the composer of *Der Freischütz* but he spoke punningly to Czerny later of the "fine piece of weaving" to be found in one of the overtures, and to Moritz Lichnowsky of the score of *Euryanthe* as overloaded with "effort."

All visitors are in agreement on the state of Beethoven's lodgings in these years. They apparently bore every resemblance to what is now presented in photographs as a "typical pad" on San Francisco's North Beach, and indeed there is something distinctly "beat" in the following wild ejaculation from Beethoven's notebooks at the time: "All that is called life shall be sacrificed to sublime art! Let me live even by means of artificial aids! If only such are to be found!" Beethoven was forever moving from place to place to escape angry landlords and recalcitrant servants. Here is a French visitor's description of one apartment:

. . . extreme dirt and disorder: pools of water decorated the floor; a rather ancient grand piano, on which dust competed for room with sheets of written or printed notes. Under it—I do not exaggerate—an unemptied chamber-pot. Beside it a small walnut table, well-accustomed to having the contents of the inkwell overturned on it. Numerous quill pens full of dried ink, compared with which the proverbial inn-pens would have been excellent. Most of the chairs had straw seats and were decorated with clothes and dishes full of the remains of the previous day's supper.

Here is another, throwing light on those pools of water:

He had always, when he had sat at his table composing for some time and felt his head heated by it, been in the habit of hurrying to the washstand, splashing pitchers of water over his heated head, and after these coolings-off, followed by only a hasty drying, to go back to work or sometimes to take a short walk in the fresh air. In what haste all this was done, so that he should not be torn from his flights of imagination, and how little care was taken to dry his soaked mop of hair, is shown by the fact that, all unknown to him, the water he had splashed over his head sometimes poured freely onto the floor, and indeed soaked through it, appearing on the ceiling of the lodgers below, and in turn occasionally led to unpleasant recriminations on the part of the latter, of the janitor, and finally of the landlord, and indeed to notice to vacate the premises.

Beethoven's two brothers, who had played little part in his life during the middle period, now enter it with a vengeance. The younger, Johann, always more remote from the composer's affections, had been a druggist in Linz for some years. He had prospered and was having an affair with his housekeeper. Beethoven heard of this and took it upon himself to intervene. He went to Linz and argued with his brother. Failing to get anywhere, he visited the Bishop, and even obtained a police order to have the girl thrown out of town. There was a violent quarrel with Johann (they had come to blows before), and the upshot of Beethoven's uncalled-for intervention was that Johann married Therese to spite him.

This was in 1812. Hardly was Beethoven back in Vienna when he precipitated a quarrel with his other brother, Karl, accusing him of stealing some of his compositions—which turned out to be in the bureau drawer. Beethoven repented when he discovered that Karl was suffering from tuberculosis, and was filled with remorse. But he seems to have transferred his suspicions to his brother's wife, Johanna. From now on she is never mentioned by him without revilement. On November 14, 1815 Brother Karl felt himself to be dying and drew up a will appointing Ludwig guardian of his nine-year-old son; a codicil reads that this guardianship, which he says he believes the composer intends to exercise in an exclusive fashion, is not to be interpreted as cutting out young Karl's mother. ". . . I recommend *compliance* to my wife and more *moderation* to my brother." The next day Karl Casper van Beethoven was dead. And within a week Beethoven had asked a doctor to make a post-mortem examination to determine whether he had been poisoned! "My poor unfortunate brother has just died," he wrote Ries in London on November 22; "he had a bad wife. . . ." There is little question whom Beethoven suspected. On November 28 he submitted an appeal to the courts to transfer the guardianship of young Karl to himself alone. On December 15 he complied with the court's request for reasons by charging Johanna with embezzle-

ment. On January 9, 1816, the court conferred sole guardianship on Beethoven and ten days later he took possession of the nephew whose miseries under his care were to cause him such ruinous torment. But for the moment, Thayer notes, Beethoven's "joy" was "unbounded."

CONTRADICTIONS

Tentative speculation is that he was and is highly intelligent, extremely insecure, ridden with repressed aggression. There are indications that he is compulsive and beset by strong, latent homosexual tendencies. . . .

Beethoven? Except for the last speculation, nothing in the above diagnosis is at variance with what we already know; and the "latent homosexual" theory has been advanced in a closely reasoned, thoroughly documented book entitled *Beethoven and His Nephew* by two Viennese psychoanalysts now residing in the United States. The quotation, however, is not from the Sterbas' book, nor does it refer to Beethoven. I clipped it from *The Nation* of August 20, 1960, and it is a description of Adolph Eichmann.

The point I would like to make before proceeding to an account of the painful relations between Beethoven and his nephew is this: complex human beings,

94

whether they be criminals or benefactors of humanity, would be nothing were they not complex. No theory of their sexual traits, real or imagined, can even begin to explain their accomplishment, or change the enormity of it in any way. An "analysis" of Eichmann would doubtless improve him in the world's eyes by revealing him to be the creature of his childhood repressions, but it would have no bearing at all on the question of why seven million innocent human beings were put to death. Similarly an "analysis" of Beethoven, though it would tend to have an opposite effect in public terms by reducing a genuine hero of humanity to a textbook-case of thwarted "normality," has as little bearing on Beethoven's accomplishment. Yet in so far as it illuminates the paradox of human character, emphasizing the fact that Beethoven's music could not have been written by a "perfect" man, and indeed exerts its tremendous power over us precisely because we feel in it Beethovn's anguish over his own imperfection, it is not without value.

In making this comparison it is not, then, my intention to imply that there is anything nefarious in such an investigation as the Sterbas made. Dana Steichen in her book on Beethoven went out of her way to ridicule and abuse the two doctors because their clinical portrait of Beethoven as a suspicious, meddling, wrong-headed, miserly and sometimes sadistic old man conflicted with her idealized image of the hero as a long-suffering martyr to true love, crucified by the willful meanness and ingratitude of a scapegoat nephew.

Mrs. Steichen follows a long line of biographers who have chosen to accept Beethoven's version of his own motives and of his nephew's character rather than present the image of a hero marred by apparently serious flaws. Schindler began the idealization by destroying 264 of the 400 volumes in which Beethoven's visitors wrote down their questions; presumably he destroyed not only those in which his own relationship with Beethoven appeared in a poor light, but those which contained material conflicting substantially with his autumnal recollection of the Master. (In later decades Schindler's calling card bore the engraved notation: *"Ami de Beethoven."*) Even the generally impartial Thayer, when he reached the point of his monumental study of Beethoven dealing with Karl, developed such fearful headaches that he was never able to complete Volumes IV and V—though the headaches interfered in no way with his subsequent work on other studies.

Mrs. Steichen not only refuses to accept Karl's childish but pitifully honest explanation of his attempted suicide—"I grew worse because my uncle wanted me to be better"—but accepts all of the composer's unjustified accusations against the boy and his mother. "It was the nephew," she says of the confused teen-ager, "who was unfit to be Beethoven's ward."

But what about the Sterbas? Are they justified in rehabilitating the reputation of the forgotten Karl and of Johanna Beethoven at the expense of our image of the immortal Ludwig, whom their massive evidence now shows to have been in these years a jealous tyrant? Does their theory that the composer in his misguided effort to be Karl's "father" was actually playing the part of a "mother"—the mother who had betrayed him in his own youth by failing to stand between him and his drunken, tyrannical father—does this theory have any validity or throw any light on the music? Must one infer, as the Sterbas do, on the basis of the flimsiest verbal evidence and the absence of positive "proof" to the contrary, that Beethoven was basically afraid of women? And is it conducive to a better understanding of Beethoven that one accept their view of his rebellious "Führer-personality" as inducing fear, "almost religious reverence" in others?

I can only answer for myself. The Freudian theories happen to leave me cold. But since the relentless pursuit of them has led the Sterbas into an investigation of questionable "facts," I am grateful to them for fresh insights along the way. I applaud their rehabilitation of Karl and Johanna. It does matter; the truth always matters, even if it comes a century late. And far from being disturbed by the evidence of a vengeful and egotistically blindered Beethoven, I am the more deeply moved by the discrepancy thus unveiled between what Beethoven tried so desperately to be and the contradictory effect his acts of heartfelt devotion had on others. But above all, I am immeasurably more impressed, after reading the Sterbas, by the resolution achieved by Beethoven in his last music. For the doctors' great mistake, perhaps their only one, is to mention the music itself. To say as they do on these few occasions that "when he [Beethoven] was achieving his last and most profound creations, his personality had changed for the worse," or that "his capacity for truth had diminished," or that "psychologically he was regressing," is not only to betray a gross misunderstanding of what is going on in the music, but to erect a wholly false dichotomy between the artist and his art.

Cabinetmaker Housekeeper

Piano-tuner

Bank Karl—

Education absolutely requires an assured course no sooner was she forbidden to see him than the opposite again

immoderate

Go with the lawyer to the Referee—

Juniper-wood

Dust broom and frying pan

Two times he went to her where he perpetrated the worst.

Since I give the money for his education to be advanced, it is natural that this end too must be gained—

Night-lights

Blankengasse

everything against her was not credited

G [iannatasio]'s letters only against me.

It is to be supposed that Smettana would not in order to spare me allow a bad thing to become worse by calling the whole thing well taken care of.

Schlemmer

Paper

to my nephew the character of his mother was never a secret, [but] this the M[agistracy] out of ill-conceived immorality and partisanship refused to acknowledge, although my nephew was instructed in the proper degree of respect for his mother

Blotting-paper

A page from the Conversation Books of 1819-1820, this one containing jottings in Beethoven's hand, reveals the turmoil of his thoughts. He is convinced that Johanna, whom he now generally refers to as the Queen of the Night, after Mozart's evil genius, is bent upon corrupting Karl. The Magistracy, at last recognizing the mother's claims, returns the guardianship to her; then the Appellate Court reverses the lower decision and awards the child back to his uncle. He tells the boy, whose boyhood is being crushed by the impossible demands of an extraordinary man, that he has no intention of bringing him up to be "ordinary." "Imitate my virtues, but not my faults," he pleads when only the faults can be apparent. Yet he knows at the same time, instinctively, that his hatred for Johanna is evil. The terrible expression of his guilt is mingled with his anguish at having to face at last the

impossibility of bringing up a child in his disorderly lodgings, of being obliged to put him in a boarding school:

Help, God! Thou seest me abandoned by all mankind, for I will not commit injustice. Hear my cry, that I may yet in the future be with my Karl, for no possibility points to it now. O hard fate! O terrible doom! No, no, my unhappy state is unending!

The first of these schools is managed by Cajetan Giannatasio del Rio, whose two daughters, Fanny and Nanny, are devoted to Beethoven. Fanny, in fact, falls in love with him; her diaries, discovered by Thayer, contain a heartbreaking picture of the distraught composer trying at the same time to supervise the education of Karl and to keep Fanny at a distance without hurting her feelings. On one occasion, knowing that she will overhear, he tells her father of the great love for a woman five years back that persists and makes him impervious to others. Fanny senses the unnatural anxiety closing in upon Karl:

98

Our dear Beethoven, whom of late we have seen for a few minutes in the presence of the Schönauers, yesterday wrote his little one a very dear letter, in which he again says so many beautiful and true things to him that it gave me real joy to read it; yet I find it not quite right that he does not let him go on living in his natural ingenuousness but requires a trust whose advantages and value the little boy is as yet quite unable to appreciate, and thus might cause him to worry if there be not something lacking in him or, in consequence of his not too strong love of truth, might even lead him to tell lies. But all this no doubt comes from his wish to furnish a substitute for his love of his mother and to be everything to him.

He tells the two girls on another occasion that he has never known of a marriage in which, after a time, one or another partner had not regretted the step. He himself, he added, more than once would have considered it the height of happiness to have married, ". . . and what a good thing it is that the wishes of mortals often remain unfulfilled."

But let us pause for a moment and summarize as factually as possible the little that is known of the objectives of Beethoven's consuming hatred and love. (That little, of course, comes filtered through the web of adulation playing about the huge shadow cast by the composer.) Thayer introduces the nephew's parents, on the eve of their marriage back in 1806, thus: "Karl van Beethoven's character and temperament were not fitted to render a wife permanently happy [Thayer throws no light on this statement elsewhere]; on the other hand his wife, before her husband's death, dishonored him by an intrigue with a medical student [no proof of this is given]; but there is no reason whatever to believe that the marriage, at the time it took place, was not considered a good one for, and by, all parties concerned." Their son was born, Thayer tells us, four months after the marriage. There is no further mention of Johanna until we find Beethoven in 1818 being accused by a village priest (in testimony filed by Johanna in court) of "encouraging his nephew to revile his mother." In the cross-examination of Karl, the boy was asked by the court if he indulged in disrespectful remarks about his mother, to which he replied that he had occasionally, in the presence of his uncle "whom he thought he would please in that way." Thayer admits that there is no proof of Johanna's moral bad character at the time Beethoven charges her with "corrupting" her son, but he does insinuate that she had been unfaithful to Karl Sr. in 1811, and Schindler (no neutral) reported years later that she gave birth to an illegitimate child while the case was pending. Her son—though he once tells Beethoven that

Johanna had been taught to steal by her father—defends his mother staunchly; for example, in this conversation with his uncle: "I do not want to hear anything derogatory to her; it is not for me to be her judge. If I were to spend the little time for which I shall be here with her it would be only a small return for all she has suffered on my account."

There is no evidence, in short, that Johanna was a bad mother, but there is considerable that she was free with her favors, and to one who idealized women as Beethoven did, such a person could not possibly be a good mother. As for Karl himself, the best evidence that he was the victim rather than the betrayer of his uncle's devotion is in the fact that he came to him sound in mind and spirit, and that after Beethoven's death he lived out a perfectly normal if undistinguished life as a good army officer and a devoted family man with five loving children.

But to return to Beethoven, was Lang thinking of his state of mind during these infertile years when he quoted the poet's "He who loves humanity learns to hate humans"? It is a half-truth that can be answered in Beethoven's case by saying that had the love ever become abstract, the hate would have conquered him and it would be all that we would hear in the music. For the time being, unquestionably, love was in full retreat in Beethoven's tormented daily existence. His possessive feeling for Karl breaks out now and again in a fit of jealousy. He resents the friendship of tutors; he suspects the headmasters of siding with Johanna. Servants bear the brunt of his temper. He suspects them of stealing from him, and fills ledgers and letters to friends with interminable accountings of the pettiest transactions. One housekeeper he calls "a frightful sow" and another he assaults with a chair. Yet always in the springs of his mind where the music rises, its terrible discords resolved by the sun of creation before they can become unstrung or bestial, the mysterious orderliness and rectitude of genius is at work. Meanwhile the fringes of consciousness repeat: I am guilty! The boy's natural desire is for his mother, and it is I, I who am depriving him: "I have sacrificed my very best for the sake of my dear Karl: bless my work, bless the widow! Why cannot I obey all the promptings of my heart and help the widow? God, God, my refuge and my rock, O my all! Thou seest my inmost thoughts, thou knowest how it hurts me to make others suffer in my good works for my dear Karl!!! O hear me, Ineffable One, hear me, thy unhappy, unhappiest of all mortals!"

100

THE MASS AND THE NINTH SYMPHONY

1823 is the *annus mirabilis* of Beethoven's Third Period, as 1806 had been of the Second. The Mass in D (*Missa Solemnis*) which had been occupying him for six years, and the Ninth Symphony which he had been bringing into focus during the latter part of this period, were completed. And if these two works are taken to be ultimate achievements in the realms of choral-religious and instrumental-secular music, the Thirty-three Variations on a Waltz by Diabelli, composed in the same year, may be regarded (together with the final piano sonata, in C minor, of the year before) as a crowning glory of the literature for the keyboard. Only the last quartets remained to be written, and while the mystical experiences expressed in them may be of a "purer" because more intimate refinement, these experiences originated in the four masterpieces of 1822–1823.

As far back as 1820 Schindler had observed the composer's struggles with the Mass. Arriving at Beethoven's lodgings in Modling that summer with a friend, he was informed by the neighbors that two servants had "escaped" the day before and that war with their temporary replacements had already been declared: "In his drawing-room, behind a locked door, we heard the Master singing, howling and stamping over the fugue for the *Credo*. After listening to this almost gruesome sound for some time, we were just about to leave when the door opened and Beethoven stood before us, a wild look on his face, which was almost terrifying. He looked as if he had just emerged victorious from a life and death struggle with the entire host of contrapuntists, his constant antagonists."

Was Schindler's conclusion one of the "punishable offenses" for which Beethoven threatened to "try" his "obtrusive appendix"? Whatever troubles counterpoint still gave the composer—and he now used it constantly—these were as nothing compared to the travail involved in matching expressively the music to the Latin text, and the deeper implications of the familiar ritual words themselves with the agonies and victories of his own experience. Beethoven was incapable of thinking of a "libretto"—even a God-given one—in any other terms.

Which is not to say that the *Missa Solemnis* is more of an artistic triumph than a devotional one. It is a triumph in both aspects. Beethoven first conceived of it (and entirely on his own initiative) as an offering to his pupil and great patron, the Archduke Rudolph, who had been appointed Cardinal-Archbishop of Olmütz.

The Mass was to be performed at the installation ceremonies of March 20, 1820. The fact that it was finished three years too late for this occasion, and that it was never put to religious use in the Empire during Beethoven's lifetime, does not mean that it was found unacceptable. The Roman Catholic Church has expressly sanctioned its performance on great occasions. But how often are a symphony orchestra, a chorus, and four solo voices capable of singing that most demanding vocal music, available? And if they were, how many worshippers would want to listen for two hours to this probing of spiritual regions beyond common experience? There are no Haydnesque periods as in Beethoven's own earlier Mass, the heroic C Major of 1807, no robust, reiterative choruses in the Handelian manner, no relaxing alternations of polyphonic severity and Italian coloratura as in the only Mass of comparable scale—Bach's B Minor. The denseness of structure and unparalleled thematic unity of the *Missa* require many hearings before the subtleties with which the text is interpreted can be grasped.

The *Gloria* starts so formidably, Tovey observes, that "had a more guileless composer worked it out normally he would not have got through it in twenty minutes" but "what happens with Beethoven is that within the compass of six bars he contrives to give a sense that this passage (bars 435-440) has gone around the universe." The effect, Miss Scott adds, "is obtained by rapid and remote modulations which obliterate the hearer's sense of key."

The *Credo,* larger still, ends with the fugue Schindler heard in gestation; but before that turbulence of joy on the phrase *et vitam venturi saeculi,* Christ's descent to earth has been described in literal cadences of unison octaves; the Virgin Birth has been accompanied by miracle-bearing strains in the Dorian mode; the Crucifixion has called forth every resource for defining pain and compassion; and the Resurrection has been announced with an electrifying burst of jubilation.

Ernest Newman sees Beethoven's Third Period initiated in the *Sanctus,* specifically in the music expressing "the central, the most mystical and esoteric moment of the ritual, the Consecration of the Host," when the voices cease and an orchestral Praeludium conveys "a curious softening and *approfondissement* of the spirit." There is certainly an anticipation of the mood of the last quartets here, and, I think,

looking forward many decades, of the mood of Wagner's *Parsifal* too. But if the five last piano sonatas do not belong to the Third Period, then one's definition of what Beethoven accomplished in the Second must become excessively broad—and a description of the Third almost esoteric.

The final section of the Mass, the *Agnus Dei,* is darker, more pessimistic in feeling than the rest, and rightly so, but it is also more personal, as though the Latin words for "sin" and "have mercy" (Beethoven had the entire text translated into German the better to study it) reopened the composer's living wounds, bringing him momentarily down out of his soaring preoccupation with eternal values into the quagmire of daily existence. The anguished cry to the Lamb of God for pity is marked (bilingually) by Beethoven *"ängstlich timidamente"* and the phrase *dona nobis pacem,* preceded by distant drum-rolls and a fanfare of trumpets in clear reference to Europe's years of agony, *"Bitte um innern und aussern Frieden"* ("a prayer for inner and outer peace"). Beethoven made so many changes in the tympani part of the score that he wore a hole in the very thick paper, his aim being, according to Thayer, to suggest the distance of the disturbers of the peace by the vagueness of the rhythms. The conclusion, Newman observes, "is enigmatic. The voices break in again with a few final ejaculations of 'pacem, pacem.' But does Beethoven really believe that the prayer will be answered, or does he leave it all as a kind of question mark projected upon the remote, indifferent sky? It is impossible to say."

There is nothing enigmatic about the conclusion to the Ninth Symphony, and in that respect only would it be possible to think of it, as Newman apparently did, as the concluding work of the Second Period. The expression of *joy* as the final residuum of any meaningful experience conceived in creative terms is, however, common to all phases of Beethoven's work. Only the very great can convince us of the aesthetic validity of "happy endings," because only they by their demonstration of capacity to suffer everything without being broken convince us that they have earned that right. All Beethoven's endings are in this sense "happy"—even the F Minor Quartet, even the *Hammerklavier* Sonata. The high-treble trills at the termination of the C Minor Sonata, ascending into some Nirvana stratosphere of white light beyond the imaginings of birds or astronauts, complement perfectly the volcanic opening movement, Beethoven's farewell to rebelliousness which he this

time labelled *"appassionata"* on his own. But the ending of the Ninth Symphony is happiest of all. We accept its happiness, once again, not because there is any of the aspect of a *deus ex machina,* relieving us of the necessity of facing more tragedy, nor because it provides a nice artistic balance to what has gone before (as might, for example, be said of the *rondo* of the *Pathétique* back in 1798) but because Beethoven convinces us by everything leading up to it that no other conclusion is possible. He even dares to drive home the point, to make it obvious, as no devious craftsman would, by directly preceding its choral paean with a short, snappy "review" in a few bars each of the three preceding movements. Shall we settle (he seems to be saying) for the tragic view, even triumphantly mastered? No! Cyclopean irony? No! Love—the most poignant expression of love ever offered? No! Even love is mortal. I will show you something implicit in all of these, but purer, more intoxicating, more irresistible!

He had had a poem of Schiller in mind for some such dimly foreseen eventuality ever since he grew up in Bonn. Sketches of the setting date from 1794, 1798, 1811 and 1822. It is not a very good poem, this *Ode to Joy,* but it was apparently always destined to be the vehicle through which words would be introduced into a symphony, for its key line "All mankind shall be as brothers" summed up succinctly Beethoven's ideal of social destiny. As if to emphasize that it is the human voices that matter, as the only possible carriers of such a message, Beethoven has the baritone lead off with three verses he interpolated on his own after wrestling daemonically with the problem of transition:

> *O Freunde, nicht diese Töne*
> *sondern lasst uns angenehmere*
> *anstimmen, und freudenvollere.*
> (*O friends, not these strains;*
> *Rather let us raise our voices*
> *And joyful be our song.*)

But the chorale rises to its most dizzying heights as human brotherhood expands to cover the universe:

> *Such' ihn überm Sternenzelt!*
> *Ueber Sternen muss er wohnen.*
> (*Seek him beyond the canopy of Heaven!*
> *He must dwell above the stars.*)

106

The Ninth Symphony was dedicated, after the usual indecision displayed by Beethoven in such matters, to the King of Prussia. Friederich Wilhelm acknowledged the honor in a perfunctory note stating that he enclosed a "diamond ring as a token of my sincere appreciation." The stone turned out to be semiprecious and the indignant Beethoven was with difficulty restrained from mailing it back.

The first performance, accompanied by parts of the Mass, was a triumph of sentiment only; the second, sixteen days later, was a disaster. The story of the deaf composer beating time after the music had stopped and having to be turned around to receive the applause is well known. The intensive rehearsing that would have been needed to give either revolutionary work a semblance of coherence did not take place. Conducting as we know it was non-existent. Singers asked to have the high, sustained notes edited and Beethoven of course refused. The critics, bearing in mind Beethoven's "endearing" early works, were polite. But when an early admirer, the composer Ludwig Spohr, confided to his diary that the choral movement was "monstrous and tasteless," confirming him in his opinion that Beethoven "was wanting in esthetic cultivation and feeling for beauty," he probably echoed the opinion of the average listener.

Beethoven, except for the thwarted prospect of money in the bank, could not have cared less. His position as the world's foremost living composer had been secure for years. Creatively, his gaze was already fixed on remoter horizons.

"MEN OF NOBLE MOULD"

Thayer quotes in full a long letter from Beethoven to the Archduke dated July 1, 1823. Perhaps he does so because it discourses so typically of business and philosophy, money and art, Earth and Heaven. To his other bodily afflictions Beethoven was now contending with the threat of blindness. As in the case of 70 out of the 105 letters addressed to his royal pupil, Beethoven was apologizing for an appointment broken—this one an appointment to correct a set of the Archduke's variations. In the first part of his letter Beethoven uses his excuse to solicit his patron's help in selling subscriptions to the Mass to various European monarchs. He apologizes for his anxiety by quoting the maxim "Necessity knows no law," and then begins his conclusion to the letter with a clear reference to the religious nebulae toward which all his music is now aspiring:

But I thank Him above the stars that I am beginning to use my eyes again. I am now writing a new symphony for England, for the Philharmonic Society, and I hope to have it completely done in a fortnight. I can not yet strain my eyes for a long period, wherefore I beg Your Imperial Highness graciously to be patient in regard to Y.I.H.'s variations which seem to me charming but need carefully to be looked through by me. Continue Y.I.H. to practice the custom of briefly jotting down your ideas at the pianoforte; for this a little table alongside the pianoforte will be necessary. By this means the fancy will not only be strengthened but one learns to fix at once the most remote ideas. It is also necessary to write without the pianoforte, and sometimes to develop a simple chorale melody now with simple, and anon with varied figurations in counterpoint and this will cause no headache to Y.I.H. but rather a great pleasure at finding yourself absorbed in the art. Gradually there comes the capacity to represent just that only which we wish to feel, an essential need in the case of men of noble mould. My eyes command me to stop, etc.

Men of noble mold . . .

Was there ever one nobler, if we listen to Beethoven speaking to us in his own language—if we contemplate the whole man and not merely the dreary extraction of social or psychic contradictions with which the historian or psychologist presents us? Religion, like art, is to the academic mind a fantasy interesting mainly for what it reveals of the "disturbed" personality. We all suffer today from this worm's-eye view of reality. But consider: is it more "real" that Beethoven loses his temper and boxes the ears of a defenseless cleaning-woman, or that at the word *adoremus* he turns his whole conscience inside-out and lays it before God in utter abnegation? Which is closer to the truth: Beethoven's confused recognition of his want of charity for failing to treat Karl's mother with anything but righteous distrust, or his mighty perception in the Mass of Christ's moment of weakness on the Cross, expressed (as Newman observes) in the soprano's sudden E-flat "and a clarinet that imposes a rending minor ninth on the supporting harmony . . . like a stab re-opening a wound"?

Only a shuttlewise Mälzel, an economic determinist or a fetishist of the couch could possibly think that the *facts* are what matters. And only an art-for-art's-sake critic or an artist enmeshed in the web of his own formal ingenuity could possibly think that the facts do *not* matter. Beethoven never made either mistake. He preferred Palestrina to all other composers of Church music, he once told a visiting organist, but it would be "folly to imitate him unless one had his genius *and his religious beliefs*" (my italics). "From the heart," he wrote at the top of the manuscript of the Mass, "may it go to the heart."

BEETHOVEN'S GOD

What exactly were Beethoven's religious beliefs? It is easier to say what they were not. After his childhood employment as organist at Bonn, I can not recall any reference in the letters or conversations to indicate that he ever entered a church again. It is notable that as he lay on his deathbed it was his friends who sent for a priest to deliver the Holy Sacrament; and Schindler reports that they begged this favor of Beethoven with considerable trepidation. He acceded readily enough and "performed his devotions with pious resignation," turning then to the company with the well-known Latin words *"Plaudite, amici, finita est comoedia!"* ("Applaud, friends, the comedy is over!"). Rabelais, after being cajoled on his deathbed into signing a will beneficial to those present, is reported to have died with the same phrase on his lips.

Was Beethoven, as some think, throughout life anti-clerical? There is no evidence of it. Was he, as many more maintain, a Protestant-under-the-skin? He seems to have had no more use for the doctrine of original sin than for the hedonistic dogma of eternal salvation as a reward for good conduct and correct observances. He was certainly devoted to Christ in his aspects of a sufferer, an outlaw, and a penitent. And he surely treats the Mass as though he intended it to speak for all Christendom. But there is no reason to suppose that he rejected the Mother Church; still less, that he set himself up as some kind of skeptic or free-thinker. Just as he appears to have been repelled by anthropomorphic concepts of a God who exists to reward or punish men—or of man striving to be *good* for any other reason than because the order of Creation requires this mark of respect for its perfection— so every world-wide manifestation of faith in a principle of divinity broad enough to encompass Man and Nature appealed to him.

Schindler reports that Beethoven kept over his desk, framed and in large letters, the following inscription from an Egyptian monument to the god Isis:

I AM THAT WHICH IS
I AM ALL, WHAT IS, WHAT WAS, WHAT WILL BE, etc.

Isis was the Egyptian goddess of the Earth, of love, of healing, of magic. Beethoven copied the inscription from an essay on Moses by Schiller. The paragraph he copied also includes the following sentences: "There is nothing more elevated than the simple grandeur with which they [i.e., the Egyptian priests] spoke of the creator of the universe. In order to distinguish him the more emphatically they gave him no name. A name, said they, is only a need for pointing a difference; he who is only, has no need of a name."

Beethoven read with great interest the Persian and Hebraic religious texts then beginning to be translated. The following passage from the Hindu sacred writings was found transcribed in his autograph:

God is immaterial: since he is invisible he can have no form, but from what we observe in his works we may conclude that he is eternal, omnipotent, omniscient, and omnipresent— The mighty one is he who is free from all desire; he alone; there is no greater than he.

Brahma; his spirit is enwrapped in himself. He, the mighty one, is present in every part of space—his omniscience is in spirit by himself and the conception of him comprehends every other one; of all comprehensive attributes that of omniscience is the greatest. For it there is no threefold existence. It is independent of everything. O God, thou art the true, eternal, blessed, immutable light of all times and all spaces. Thy wisdom embraces thousands upon thousands of laws, and yet thou dost always act freely and for thy honor. Thou wert before all that we revere. To thee be praise and adoration. Thou alone art the truly blessed one (Bhagavan); thou, the essence of all laws, the image of all wisdom, present throughout the universe, thou upholdest all things.

Sun, ether, Brahma [these words are crossed out].

VARIATIONS AND REVERBERATIONS

The third musical landmark of the *annus mirabilis*, the Thirty-three Variations on a Theme by Diabelli, began as a musical joke. When asked to contribute a single variation to a set of thirty-two composed by as many hands, Beethoven took a quick look at the bouncy dance-hall tune by this "Diabolus" of a music publisher who had not long ago threatened to sue him in a dispute over the Mass, and snorted, "It's a Schusterfleck!"—a cobbler's patch. But his irrepressible humor and imagination got the better of this judgment, and he asked Diabelli how much he would be willing to pay for not one but *thirty-three* variations, which of course would have to be printed as a separate book. The publisher said "80 ducats," and within a matter of months he had received what turned out to be the companion-piece to Bach's exhaustive "Art of Fugue." Every imaginable spell was cast upon Diabelli's tune, including along the way musical compliments to Bach, Handel, Haydn and Mozart.

Disagreement still rages over whether the ordinariness of the waltz was a help or a hindrance. Tovey has this to say:

110

Diabelli's theme has often been cited as a proof that Beethoven could make the most enormous works out of nothing. This is not true. He could not have made an enormous set of variations out of the sublime themes which he treats in variation form in his sonata works. Diabelli's theme is as prosaic as the hard-shell businessman who wrote it, but it does mean business, and a stronger structure has never been realized in reinforced concrete. It is a theme which sets the composer free to build recognizable variations in every conceivable way.

Among the thirty-two contributors to Diabelli's less exalted anthology were the twenty-five-year-old Franz Schubert and the twelve-year-old Franz Liszt. Since Liszt's own account of his meeting with Beethoven in 1823 is vivid and is not included in Thayer or any other biography that I know of, I include it here in full:

I was about eleven years old when my respected teacher Czerny took me to see Beethoven. Already a long time before, he had told Beethoven about me and asked him to give me a hearing some day. However, Beethoven had such an aversion to infant prodigies that he persistently refused to see me. At last Czerny, indefatigable, persuaded him, so that, impatiently, he said: "Well, bring the rascal to me, in God's name!" It was about ten o'clock in the morning when we entered the two small rooms in the *Schwarzspanierhaus*, where Beethoven was living at the time, myself very shy, Czerny kind and encouraging. Beethoven was sitting at a long, narrow table at the window, working. For a time he scrutinized us grimly, exchanged a few hurried words with Czerny and remained silent when my good teacher called me to the piano. The first thing I played was a short piece by Ries.

When I had finished Beethoven asked me whether I could play a fugue by Bach. I chose the fugue in C minor from the Well-Tempered Clavier. "Could you also transpose this fugue at once into another key?" Beethoven asked me. Fortunately, I could. After the final chord, I looked up. The Master's darkly glowing gaze was fixed upon me penetratingly. Yet suddenly a benevolent smile broke up his gloomy features, Beethoven came quite close, bent over me, laid his hand on my head and repeatedly stroked my hair. "Devil of a fellow!" he whispered, "such a young rascal!" I suddenly plucked up courage. "May I play something of yours now?" I asked cheekily. Beethoven nodded with a smile. I played the first movement of the C major Concerto. When I had ended, Beethoven seized both my hands, kissed me on the forehead and said gently: "Off with you! You're a happy fellow, for you'll give happiness and joy to many other people. There is nothing better or greater than that!"

This event in my life has remained my greatest pride, the palladium of my whole artistic career. I speak of it only very rarely and only to my intimate friends.

Richard Wagner was one year younger than Liszt, and was beginning to be familiar with Beethoven's work in 1823, but the "palladium" of his career as an artist was his discovery of the Ninth Symphony about five years later. His account of this discovery as he tells it in his autobiography is equally characteristic:

Beethoven's Ninth Symphony became the mystical goal of all my strange thoughts and desires about music. I was first attracted to it by the opinion prevalent among musicians, not only in Leipzig but elsewhere, that this work had been written by Beethoven when he was already half mad. It was considered the *non plus ultra* of all that was fantastic and incomprehensible, and this was quite enough to rouse in me a passionate desire to study this mysterious work. At the very first glance at the score, of which I obtained possession with such difficulty, I felt irresistibly attracted by the long-sustained pure fifths with which the first phrase opens: these chords, which, as I related above, had played such a supernatural part in my childish impressions of music, seemed in this case to form the spiritual keynote of my own life. This, I thought, must surely contain the secret of all secrets, and accordingly the first thing to be done was to make the score my own by a process of laborious copying. I well remember that on one occasion the sudden appearance of the dawn made such an uncanny impression on my excited nerves that I jumped into bed with a scream as though I had seen a ghost. The symphony at that time had not yet been arranged for the piano; it had found so little favor that the publisher did not feel inclined to run the risk of producing it. I set to work at it, and actually composed a complete piano solo, which I tried to play to myself. I sent my work to Schott, the publisher of the score, at Mainz. I received in reply a letter saying "that the publishers had not yet decided to issue the Ninth Symphony for the piano, but that they would gladly keep my laborious work," and offered me remuneration in the shape of the score of the great *Missa Solemnis* in D, which I accepted with great pleasure.

CRISIS

The tragedy of love misdirected, unwanted, spurned, was meanwhile unfolding in Vienna, sweeping Karl inexorably to the attempt upon his life that was to bring him release and, just as inexorably, sweeping Beethoven, the man, to his earthly doom.

The love to which every witness in the years 1824–1825 testifies is most touchingly described in a contemporary reminiscence unavailable to Thayer and unquoted by subsequent biographers: "His love for his nephew must also be mentioned as manifest proof of his goodness of heart. As a lioness fights for possession of her young, so he strove for the happiness of influencing the boy's upbringing, which, it seems, had for some time not been in the best hands. His eyes shone with joy when he looked at him; all the love in his rich and deep nature seemed to concentrate on this one object. The most tender father can take no more interest in his son's development than did Beethoven in the progress of his nephew." Thayer documents thoroughly the mercurial fluctuations of this great love as it broke in waves upon the naturally resisting fleshly barriers of its object, tumbling back in the face of the incredulous lover. A letter to Karl of June 9, 1825 is filled with forebodings: ". . . the cold weather . . . solitude weakens me still more, for my weakness often borders on a swoon. O do not pain me more! The man with the scythe will not give me much more time." On September 14 he envisions his own death more clearly: "God has never deserted me. Somebody will be found who will close my eyes."

He writes in a margin of the Conversation Books a title for a composition: "On the Death of Beethoven." But still he alternately nurses the nineteen-year-old "boy" and accuses him of the basest ingratitude. In his own words, Beethoven is now "filled with anxiety." He threatens, pleads, cries out for mercy:

If you find me violent, ascribe it to my great concern for yourself, beset as you are by many dangers.

I hope at least to receive a letter from you tomorrow. Do not make me fear. O, think of my sufferings! By good right I ought to have no cares of this kind; but what have I not experienced!

Reflect that I am sitting here and might easily fall ill.

God is my witness, I dreamed only of being rid of you and of this miserable brother and the hideous family which he foisted upon me. God hear my prayer for I can *never* trust you again.

Unfortunately your father—or rather, not your father.

Now he begs for forgiveness—fearing the worst:

My precious son:

Go no further—Come but to my arms, not a harsh word shall you hear. O God, do not rush me to destruction. . . . You shall be received lovingly as ever. What to consider, what to do in the future—this we will talk over affectionately. On my word of honor no reproaches, since they would in no case do good now. Henceforth you may expect from me only the most loving care and help. Do but come. Come to the faithful heart of your father.

BEETHOVEN.

[He adds a postscript in disheveled French:]

Come home at once on getting this.

Si vous ne viendres pas vous me tuerés surement lisès la lettre et restés a la maison chez vous, venes de m'embrasser votre pere vous vraiment adonné soyes assurés, que tout cela resterá entre nous.

[on the margin:] Only for God's sake come back today. It might bring you, who knows what danger. Hurry, hurry!

He bares his lacerated heart, pouring out his love—as in the Mass, under an "indifferent sky": "Do come—do not permit *my poor heart to bleed longer*" (Beethoven's italics).

He hears that Karl has again committed the unmentionable offense. He has secretly visited the Queen of the Night:

Till now only suspicions, although I have received assurances from one that there is again secret intercourse between you and your mother. Am I again to experience the most abominable ingratitude? No; if the bond is broken, be it so. You will make yourself hated by all impartial persons who hear of this ingratitude. . . . I ought not to mix into these miserable affairs. If the pact oppresses you then in God's name—I leave you to Divine Providence. I have done my duty and am ready to appear before the Supreme Judge. Do not fear to come to me tomorrow. As yet I only suspect—God grant that *nothing* be true, for your misfortune would truly be incalculable indifferently as the rascally brother and possibly your—mother would take it.

On Saturday, July 29, Beethoven called Holz (Schindler for the moment was in disfavor) and told him that he had reason to fear the worst. Holz went to the school, found Karl, and also in a drawer a loaded pistol. When he asked the boy why he thought to kill himself, Karl muttered something about "debts" and excused himself to get some papers. He did not return. Holz reported back to Beethoven and there is an entry in the latter's hand in the Conversation Books: "He will drown himself."

Meanwhile Karl had gone to a pawnbroker, hocked his watch, and left with a new pistol. He drove out of the city, spent the night writing letters, and on Sunday morning in the ruins of Rauhenstein shot himself in the head. A teamster found him lying there, wounded but conscious enough to give his mother's address where he was carried directly. When Beethoven arrived, Karl's first words were: "It is done. . . . Do not plague me with reproaches and lamentations." Beethoven's reply is not recorded. As soon as he had left, the boy threatened to tear the bandages from his temple if another word was spoken to him about his uncle.

Beethoven was shocked, of course, and perhaps momentarily chastened, but anyone who might expect him to have admitted that he was *wrong* would entertain the supposition that he never had felt sure of being *right*—and that all the certainty in his music could have been founded on self-doubt. Beethoven, to be sure, was filled with humility at the thought of his own sinfulness, and even at his want of charity as regards Johanna. But to expect that he now be permitted to see that Karl's near self-destruction was the direct result of a love that filled his whole being would be to ask that he become an embodiment of reason, a psychoanalyst, or a saint. Being only a great artist, and the most vulnerable of human beings, he turned to Stephan Breuning and said: ". . . the disgrace that he has brought upon me! And I loved him so!"

116

DEATH

Schindler says that the blow was so great that Beethoven's back became bent and he began to look like a man of seventy. He listened in utter disbelief to Holz's report of what Karl had told the police: "He said that he was tired of life because he saw in it something different from what you wisely and righteously could." He had been "weary of imprisonment," Karl told the magistrate. "I grew worse because my uncle wanted me to be better." Hatred he neither expressed nor felt, but the fear was obvious.

Beethoven, who was still opposed to Karl's returning to his mother, even for a day, took Breuning's advice and began to pull strings to secure him a cadetship in the regiment of Fieldmarshal Baron Stutterheim. But meanwhile, to allow time for the young man's hair to grow and cover his wound, the composer accepted the offer of his brother Johann that they both spend a few weeks at Gneixendorf. Beethoven, always sensitive to the suggestion of words, remarked that the name "sounds like the breaking of an axle-tree."

At first the visit seemed to have a calming effect on Beethoven's nerves. He completed his last compositions, the serene F Major Quartet and the new (happy) ending to the great B-flat Major Quartet of the year before. Karl seems to have enjoyed the country life thoroughly, for soon Beethoven is upbraiding him for his unwillingness to return to Vienna. Karl's answer, in the Conversation Books, is querulous but it indicates that he has no intention of giving up his hard-earned freedom:

If you want to go, good; if not, good again. But I beg of you once more not to torment me as you are doing; you might regret it, for I can endure much, but not too much. You treated your brother in the same way today without cause. You must remember that other people are also human beings.—These everlasting unjust reproaches!—Why do you make such a disturbance? Will you let me go out a bit today? I need recreation. I'll come again later.—I only want to go to my room.—I am not going out. I want only to be alone for a little while.—Will you not let me go to my room?

Soon quarrelling with Johann and his wife broke out. Beethoven outraged his brother with a suggestion that he disinherit his own wife and leave his estate to Karl. One evening, in a rage, Beethoven decided to return to Vienna at once.

It is surprising that the scene that now took place has led no one to draw a parallel between Beethoven and King Lear. Because of the quarrel with Johann, the frenzied autocrat who believed himself the victim of filial ingratitude either refused or was denied the ordinary transportation. He hitched a ride in a milk-wagon. It was a raw, stormy night and his clothes as usual were in dilapidated condition. He was forced to spend the night in a tavern, the room unheated and without shutters. Toward midnight he was seized with fever-chills, a violent thirst, and pains in the side—the first symptoms of the illness from which he was never to recover. He arrived exhausted in Vienna on December 2. Dr. Wawruch, the first of a series of physicians to treat him during the remainder of his life, paid his first visit to the *Schwarzspanierhaus* on December 5. "A violent rage," he wrote years later, "a great grief because of ingratitude and undeserved humiliation, was the cause of the mighty explosion."

The four months that follow were a nightmare of diseases compounded by conflicting diagnoses and neglectful treatment. Pneumonia, cirrhosis of the liver, diarrhoea, dropsy, syphilis, jaundice, are only half a dozen of the conditions suggested. Beethoven's legs and belly became enormously swollen and he was tapped four times to relieve the pain. He was given sweat-baths and frozen punches, juniperberry tea, champagne, caraway seeds, and God knows what else.

He never lost his humor. "Professor," he said to Dr. Seibert as the water spurted out from one of the incisions, "you remind me of Moses striking the rock with his staff!" Holz and Schindler alternated in carrying final messages. Karl, preparing for his military career, came once and gave his uncle a lesson in simple multiplication. He rededicated the C-sharp Minor Quartet to Baron Stutterheim. A gift of the forty volumes of Dr. Arnold's edition of Handel gave him great pleasure. The London Philharmonic Society sent him a generous advance against

a symphony they knew he would never write. He wrote a consoling note to Zmeskall, confined with gout. Wegeler and Eleanora wrote him a cheering letter from Bonn. Twelve bottles of Rüdesheimer Berg arrived from Frankfort. Franz Schubert was warmly received. Stephan von Breuning's young son, Gerhard, showed him a picture of Haydn's birthplace and Beethoven exclaimed: "In so small a house so great a man was born!" Indeed it was Gerhard (to whom he now transferred the old nickname for Karl, "Trouser Button") whose visits gave him the most pleasure. Gerhard alone spoke to him frankly, as an equal, without any sense that he was addressing either a genius or a madman. And judging by twenty volumes of children's stories that turned up in the inventory later, Beethoven must have read to him.

It is ironical that Beethoven's maligned sister-in-law, Therese, was one of the two persons attending him when he died on the afternoon of March 26, 1827. The other, Anselm Hüttenbrenner, left the following description from which I have omitted only some of the interpretative rhetoric:

Frau van Beethoven and I only were in the death-chamber during the last moments of Beethoven's life. After Beethoven had lain unconscious, the death-rattle in his throat from three o'clock in the afternoon till after five, there came a flash of lightning accompanied by a violent clap of thunder, which garishly illuminated the death-chamber. (Snow lay before Beethoven's dwelling.) After this unexpected phenomenon of nature, which startled me greatly, Beethoven opened his eyes, lifted his right hand and looked up for several seconds with his fist clenched and a very serious, threatening expression. . . . When he let the raised hand sink to the bed, his eyes closed. . . .

Breuning and Schindler had been at the cemetery selecting a plot. With Johann and Holz they began the search for the missing bank-shares, Karl's well-preserved fortune. Brother Johann (most Beethovenishly) infuriated the others by hinting that their search was a sham. The secret drawer, containing also the other documents and miniatures, was finally located by Holz.

The funeral took place on the afternoon of March 29. All the schools in the capital were closed. Twenty thousand people jammed the square in front of the *Schwarzspanierhaus*. A *Miserere* from the *Equali* for Trombones was sung. Schubert and Czerny were among the torchbearers. The funeral march from the A-flat Major Sonata was heard as the procession passed the Rothes Haus. Grillparzer delivered the funeral oration: "Whoever comes after him will not be able to continue, he will have to begin again, for his predecessor ended only where art itself must end."

Coda

"BRIGHT THINGS OF HEAVEN"

O carne, o sangue, o legnio, o doglia strema,
Giusto per vo' si facci el mie peccato,
Di ch'i'pur naqqui, e tal fu'l padre mio.
Tu sol se' buon: la tuo pietà suprema
Soccorra al mie preditto iniquio stato;
Si presso a morte, e sì lontan da Dio.
(O flesh, O blood, O cross, last agony,
Redeem, O all of you, my sin, which came
Into my body through my father's blood.
Christ, you alone are good. O turn to me!
With all your boundless pity cleanse my shame,
So close to death and still so far from God.)

How excellent an epitaph and soul's biography! In true humility—and pride so great it recognizes no superior but the Divine Son—how close to Beethoven! And rightly so. For these are the words of a kindred spirit, endowed as greatly, as mortally stricken and abused, as alone with God. Living in as disorderly a squalor, penurious, as physically ruined, cantankerous to the end, possessed by love but never possessing, Michelangelo summed up in another three lines of verse, fragmented like his marbles, the willful destiny of both men to turn transient heartache into imperishable joy:

Con tanta servitù, con tanto tedio,
E con falsi concetti e gran periglio
Dell'alma, a scolpir qui cose divine.

(With so much servitude, with so much anguish
And with false concepts perilling my soul,
Sculpt I must, here on earth, bright things of heaven.)

For some reason, the longer he lived—and he lived thirty years longer than Beethoven—the less Michelangelo was able to finish. This torment, at least, was spared Beethoven. His final compositions are not only complete works of art, finished in every detail, but in advance of anything the artist attempted before, even in the Ninth Symphony or the Mass in D. Grillparzer was right. Artists would have to begin again, finding new passageways to the ever-hidden lode of truth; but never again would they be without the testimony of what complex treasure a simple heart may mine from it.

Paradoxical? Of course. Art is a paradox. The Pharisees pointed this up, assuming they were dealing with no God but a journeyman in the healing profession: *He saves others, himself he cannot save*. All evils and afflictions, Beethoven recognized, "are mysterious and all the greater, indeed, more popular, the more one discusses them with others; easier to endure only inasmuch as that which we fear becomes common property." Yes, Beethoven is always aware of the discrepancy between what he is and what he makes, with no apologies for the first. "I cannot love anything that is not beautiful," he writes Gleichenstein, "else I should love myself." And to Therese Brunswick: "An eagle looked up at the sun, that was it, I cannot forget it. But do not imagine that such a thing makes me think of myself."

Is the simple man who tells Marie Bigot "I am always most natural with my friends, detesting every kind of inhibition" the same who writes in his notebook "Never overtly show all men the contempt they deserve, for one can never know when one may need them"? Of course! Had Beethoven followed this advice he gives himself in a moment of cynicism, he would not have been Beethoven. He could no more hide his contempt than his love. His crude attempts to be Machiavellian with publishers fooled no one. And if not one of his friends was permanently estranged by the way he sometimes permitted this petty contempt to show, shall we make the error of separating the nobility in the music from that in the man? Beethoven had "paranoid" tendencies, certainly, as artists probably always will have so long as societies fail to place art on at least an equal footing with money-lending and *haute couture*. But to think that Beethoven for one moment placed art in a different weighing-scale from life is to miss the whole meaning of his music. "I know of no excellencies in people other than those which make them count among better men." And again: "Like all the arts, music is founded on the exalted symbols of the moral sense: all true invention is a moral progress."

This is the place to look a little further into the difference between the "middle" Beethoven and the "late." Might one describe it as the difference, philosophically speaking, between duality and mysticism? The works of the Second Period are essentially efforts to resolve through art conflicts between personality and social determinism, freedom and necessity, good and evil, life and the spirit. The confrontations are dramatic and the resolutions are the outcome of opposition. Beethoven had changed greatly. "My art shall be exhibited only in the service of the poor," he had written to Wegeler in 1801. The self-deception and lack of humility implicit in such a remark belong to the young revolutionary. The young revolutionary could have been arrested for intimacy with the enemy, but was not —thanks to his almost exclusive circle of aristocratic friends. The old penitent *was* arrested—in 1821, *as a tramp*; he was released only when the police were convinced that the disreputable figure was none other than—Beethoven. The point is not that it is better to be arrested as a vagrant than as a purposeful reformer, but that in 1821 Beethoven, as an artist, was all of a piece. Gone was the pose, the attitude, the deliberate attempt to impose a solution upon a problem by an act of will. The will remains—Beethoven's music never becomes passive—but it is one with the will of nature.

The conflict was hammered out—the act is implicit in the title as well as the music—in the *Hammerklavier* Sonata (Opus 106). As was often the case with Beethoven, whose sketch-books should some day be edited and tape-recorded as an unparalleled revelation of creative continuity, a great work received its trial run in a lesser one. Just as the chattering violence of the "Waldstein" Sonata's opening had been anticipated in the seventh Bagatelle of Opus 33, so the *Hammerklavier's* slow movement seems to have germinated in the third Bagatelle of the Opus 126 set, although this piece was published in final form much later. (The "classical" fughetta, incidentally, which Beethoven introduces as a kind of reminiscent haven of tranquility in the very middle of the mammoth closing fugue of the *Hammer-klavier* could be a deliberate tribute to Bach, recalling as it does the fughetta in the seventh Prelude of the *Well-Tempered Clavier*.) Throughout this most revolutionary of Beethoven's works, in fact, the past and the future meet, as on a battlefield. At moments such unleashed savagery rises to the surface as was not to be heard for ninety-five years, when Stravinsky, in *Le Sacre*, invoked Africa. And one is not surprised in 1960 to hear the ideological guide to the musical avant-garde in Paris confer the ultimate tribute upon a protegé by stating that he has written the most original piano composition since the *Hammerklavier*.

The *Hammerklavier* Sonata is unresolved, but it is not dualistic. Its fugue does not "answer" the pounding anxiety of the first movement or the despair of the long *Adagio*; it simply restates these residues of Beethoven's darkest days, his four-years' dearth, in terms of polyphonic *energy*.

The *Hammerklavier* Sonata is not the work of a mystic, but all the great works that follow it are. For the abandonment of ego that is involved in decompartmentalizing such human reactions to a tragic life as "despair" or "joy," "rejection" or "acceptance," and translating intellectual energy into the composite picture of a whole experience, could only be accomplished by a total identification of the creative personality with the cosmos.

THE LAST QUARTETS

1823, the *annus mirabilis,* was over. Fourteen years had elapsed since Beethoven had written a quartet, the sombre F Minor one of 1810.

The first of the last five, that in E-flat Major, was completed in 1824 but probably begun two years earlier. It seems to grow out of some of the more acutely mystical moods of the Mass, the mood of the orchestral Praeludium to the *Sanctus* for example—moods demanding the greater refinement and intimacy of the quartet medium for further exploration.

The color of the opening movement, though marked *Maestoso* and commencing as sombrely as the F Minor Quartet, is radiant. "La Gaieté" Beethoven scrawled over a sketch for it in his notebooks. The "singing" slow movement that follows is a set of variations, and a very long set, on an ascending theme. "One seems to have lingered," Schumann was to write of it, "not fifteen short minutes but an eternity." The third movement, *Scherzando,* is almost as complex and long. The Finale, reminiscent of the old rondo conclusions, swings in its own indescribable fashion. This was music as passionate and—who will deny it?—more deeply searching than any yet composed. Yet this E-flat Major Quartet, with its conventional four-movement pattern and obeisance to what has gone before, gives only the *tone* of what is to come. It is appropriate where it is, for Beethoven, perhaps alone among great artists, seems to have thought of particular works in relation to all the others —witness the alternation of "big" and "little" symphonies, the welcome cadence of the "gentle" sonatas of Opuses 78 and 90 between the stormy middle and late ones.

Beethoven's continuing capacity to learn—even from the lowliest of talents— is demonstrated by a story Thayer had from a performer at one of the rehearsals of this quartet:

128

At the close of the last movement of the quartet there occurred a *meno vivace* which seemed to me to weaken the general effect. At the rehearsal, therefore, I advised that the general tempo be maintained, which was done, to the betterment of the effect. Beethoven, crouched in a corner, heard nothing, but watched with strained attention. After the last stroke of the bows he said, laconically, "Let it be so," went to the desks and crossed out the *meno vivace* in the four parts.

Which is not to infer that Beethoven at this late date, or at any earlier date, was unsure of his judgment. The process of trial-and-error, in his case, was simply never-ending. From boyhood on, he had been in the habit of putting the most rudimentary of ideas on paper. The method of composition was laborious, and right up to publication subject to change. No other composer of his rank wrote so little. But the excessive time, in many cases extending over years, devoted to clarifying a theme that now sounds perfectly "spontaneous" was never wasted in backward motion. "I change many things," he had told a fellow-composer the year before. "I discard and try again until I am satisfied. Then, however, there begins in my head the development in every direction and, inasmuch as I know exactly what I want, the fundamental idea never deserts me; it arises before me, grows. I see and hear, and the picture in all its extent and dimensions stands before my mind in a single projection, and there remains for me nothing but the labor of writing it down."

The next three quartets are less accessible in their communication than the first and the last. They are also more radical in their means. Prince Galitzen (who commissioned two of them, along with the E-flat Major, but did not pay for all three until years after Beethoven's death) wrote the composer from Russia: "Your genius is centuries in advance and at the present time there is scarcely one hearer who would be sufficiently enlightened to enjoy the full beauty of this music, but posterity will pay homage to you and bless your memory." The middle three, Marion Scott writes:

. . . have become the testament of modern music. From them derive the methods which Wagner expanded to such glorious purpose in his *Ring, Tristan* and *Parsifal*; in them may be found the principles of César Franck's thematic metamorphosis and cyclic development; in the bare, sparing technique of Beethoven's last F major Quartet is the presage of Bartók. Stravinsky and all the schools of economists; in the *Grosse Fuge* is the triumphant assertion of linear counterpoint.

The A Minor Quartet was written more or less simultaneously with the B-flat,

130

one movement of the latter having been intended (it is believed) for the former. The first movement of the A Minor is long, full of plaints in the spirit of the old F Minor, but with the difference that whenever these plaints become unbearably dissident they receive "healing" ministrations from a second theme which is in a major key. The "German Dance" of the next movement is wildly ill-described by either word, being neither German in any local sense, nor danceable. (George Ballanchine, the great choreographer, recognized the intractable character of *all* Beethoven's music for interpretative purposes when he told an interviewer once: "I can read almost any Beethoven piece, but I cannot *see* anything being danced to it. Beethoven's music represents something . . . and people like to put themselves into that picture. . . . Mozart, Stravinsky and Webern—that is a different kind of music. . . . The music of men like Beethoven and Brahms accommodates the individual because you can find a reflection of your personal feelings in it.")

The overwhelming third movement of the A Minor begins like a Victoria motet: lofty, liturgical, impassioned. Beethoven wrote over its score *"Heiliger Dankgesang eines Genessenen an die Gottheit, in der Lydischen Tonart"* (Song of Thanksgiving to the Deity by a Convalescent, in the Lydian Mode) and over its soaring yet intimate concluding section: *"Mit innigster Empfindung"* (With the most inner feeling). Music as therapy . . . in the decade that had passed since Dorothea Ertmann's sonata this way of writing had become second nature. "If I could give as definite expression to my thoughts about my illness," Beethoven had once remarked to Amalie Sebold at Teplitz, "as I can to my thoughts in music, I would soon cure myself!" Here now, a decade later, there must have been one "sound" that Beethoven could never escape. The music's throb and pulse subside, leaving nothing audible over the faintly perceptible flow of the bloodstream but the heartbeats themselves—as if this organ alone, after the baser parts of man's anatomy have ceased to function, must continue to operate, filling the universe at last with its echoes. The veiled radiance of the plain-song is punctuated by emphatic affirmations of faith, *sforzato;* then the dissonant rapture of the chant continues to a final whispering *diminuendo.*

The finale is marked *Alla Marcia, assai vivace; Allegro appassionato.* There is a place in its commanding progress that could be cited to characterize Beethoven's essential soundness better than any other single passage. In Yeats' words, "things fall apart"; total chaos threatens for a moment—as in that opening of the Ninth Symphony that gave such a *frisson* to susceptible Wagner—yet sanity and order are restored somehow by Beethoven's superior will. No Wagnerian descent into luxurious physicality or devitalizing self-pity is permitted. Work, action, confidence in the restorative powers of body, mind, and spirit, working *together* in normal harmony, save the day. It is interesting to know that this finale was actually intended for the Ninth Symphony by Beethoven; it is reminiscent of the Ninth throughout.

The next quartet, in point of time of composition, is the B-flat (Opus 130). Abandoning over-all sonata form entirely, it is in six movements, and the six are closely related. They are facets, one might say, of the same root experience. The opening movement, a dialogue between a tragic *Adagio* and a mad *Allegro,* contains no less than fifteen changes of tempo. The conversational breaks are not merely impatient, they are jolting; and needless to say neither party "wins." A bridging movement marked *Presto,* lasting for one hundred seconds and irresistibly syncopated in its middle section (Trio), separates the opening movement from a more stately, even-tempered dialogue. There are echoes, *pizzicato,* on the plucked strings. Long, moaning complaints from the violins are punctuated by ruffled bursts of impatience in the bass, yet toward the end these inharmonious voices somehow merge and in the very process of their unwilling but energetic cooperation dissipate the mood of ill-health. At the end there is a spirit of elation—the kind of brisk, lilting, slightly unreal elation one feels leaving the reality of a hospital sickbed for the unreality of a homecoming celebration.

The fourth movement is in "German dance" style again, strongly bowed, rustic, Brueghelish, but withal grave. This is not the nature-lover in Beethoven who said "Every tree in the countryside said to me 'Holy! Holy!' "—the Beethoven of the *Heiligedankgesang.* Rather it is the Beethoven whose favorite word was *aufgeknöpft* (unbuttoned); the Beethoven who groused to Gerhardt von Breuning in the park about the shrubs clipped French-style to resemble a wall: "All artifice! Docked like old farthingales! I only feel well when surrounded by wild scenery...." It is the Beethoven who loved taverns filled with brawling countrymen and who, seated in one once, had laughed uproariously after flinging a plate of gravy at the waiter, forgetting, as Beethoven condemned-to-life so often did, that freedom and

equality in this world have still to be won, and that the waiter would not be permitted to fling back.

The whimsical, Haydnesque German dance comes to an end. "A great upsurge of good feelings," Beethoven once confessed to Bettina, "often drives me back into myself all the more violently." The *Alla tedesca* is followed at once by the justly famous *Cavatina*, a grave, unadorned song of unutterable sadness. The miracle of this movement is not that it contains so much of grief, but that it conveys it—even to the sobs and wracking silences—without a trace of sentimentality. The form is so simple that even a child instantly grasps its meaning and feels something akin to pity for the great heart in such torment. Nothing Beethoven ever wrote so moved him, Holz recalled; "Merely to revive it afterwards in his thoughts and feelings brought forth renewed tributes of tears." When Holz suggested that this was perhaps the greatest of all the quartets, Beethoven replied: "Each in its way. Art demands of us that we shall not stand still. You will find a new manner of voice treatment [part-writing] and, thank God! there is *less lack of fancy than ever before*." But afterwards Beethoven declared that the C-sharp Minor Quartet was his favorite.

The *Cavatina* is followed by a "sadly gay" yet jubilant finale, written by Beethoven at Gneixendorf to replace the original conclusion, an immense fugue which the taste of the time (and of our time, still) found unwieldy. Without attempting to verbalize its profoundly intellectual burden, I would describe the *Grosse Fuge* as a single, sixteen-minute-long sustained climax; a crisis, in a perpetual state of being resolved; the anatomy of *becoming*. The fugue's stridencies grated on most ears for a hundred years, seeming to confirm the judgments of Albrechtsberger and other teachers that in this medium Beethoven was as floundering as a beached whale. Holz may have cited their judgments when Beethoven said to him: "To make a fugue requires no great skill—in my student days I made dozens of them. But today imagination asserts its rights, and a new and truly poetic element must be introduced into the traditional form." Sullivan gives voice to the feeling of awe which the Great Fugue now inspires:

The fugue has been called an expression of the reconciliation of freedom and necessity, or of assertion and submission, and the terms may pass because they suggest the state of consciousness that informs the fugue, a state in which the apparently opposing elements of

134

life are seen as necessary and no longer in opposition. Beethoven had come to realize that his creative energy, which he at one time opposed to his destiny, in reality owed its very life to that destiny. It is not merely that he believed that the price was worth paying; he came to see it as necessary that a price should be paid. To be willing to suffer in order to create is one thing; to realize that one's creation necessitates one's suffering, that suffering is one of the greatest of God's gifts, is almost to reach a mystical solution of the problem of evil, a solution that it is probably for the good of the world that very few people will ever entertain.

Whether a very few or many have achieved sufficient grace to comprehend the next stage in Beethoven's development, the quartet that he himself regarded as his greatest, is a moot point. For years after Beethoven's death the C-sharp Minor—the one re-dedicated to Fieldmarshal Stutterheim following Karl's attempted suicide—was ignored or decried. None of the modern commentators, learned or illumined, admit to difficulties. One wonders. To comprehend any art one must first be "sent" by it. I confess that neither the opening fugue nor the celebrated *Andante* variations break me up, and I am perfectly sure that the fault is not Beethoven's. Surely one of the difficulties involved is in that precarious balance between mourning and celebration so often cited. Another is in the subtle "recall" of motives from the A Minor and B-flat quartets—a device testified to by Beethoven himself when he alarmed the publisher by describing the C-sharp Minor as "cribbed together variously from this and that." My ear is not good enough to enjoy or to detect this echoing unless I stop the record and laboriously compare one such passage with another. But I am wholly in rapport again with the fifth movement's *Presto*, a humor as infectious as Cervantes' told in terms of syncopated tilts with windmills, *ritardandos,* inebriated gasps for breath and Puckish *pizzicati*. The nobility of the twenty-eight-measure *Adagio* that follows is not open to question; nor the hurtling frenzied ecstasy of the concluding *Allegro*—the only one of the seven movements in sonata-form. For the essential message of the C-sharp Minor Quartet I defer to Sullivan who has made its mysteries his particular province:

Our experience of the opening fugue . . . is surely one of the most pregnant and exalted that we know. Yet Wagner described this movement as the greatest expression of melancholy in all music. One may understand him saying this, and yet be utterly unable to agree with him. That he heard more than melancholy in the movement we may be convinced, but for the something more he had no words. And yet the presence of that something more makes his description not only inadequate, but entirely erroneous. What is communicated to us in the first movement of the C sharp Minor quartet has no more to do with melancholy than it has to do with joy. All art exists to communicate states of consciousness which are higher synthetic wholes than those of ordinary experience, but in these last quartets Beethoven is dealing with states for which there are no analogues in any other art. Regarding the content of some of his earlier work he could refer a questioner to Shakespeare. Regarding the content of these works he could refer him to nobody. . . .

In the light of this experience we arrive in the next movement, as a new-born creature in a new world. The virginal purity of this movement, its etherial and crystalline quality, suggests to us a spirit not yet made flesh. . . .

In these moments of illumination Beethoven had reached that state of consciousness that only the great mystics have ever reached, where there is no discord. And in reaching it he follows an outbreak of the most exultant gaiety. There is no trace in the Scherzo of anything but the purest joy. Its most human quality is its humor, but humor so carefree and radiant is scarcely human. The adagio introduction to the finale has all the quality of a sorrowful awakening. It is as if the whole of the quartet preceding this movement had been a dream. But that, we are passionately convinced, cannot be true. The note of complete authenticity in that opening fugue cannot be mistaken. But it is certain that there is a withdrawal of the vision. It signifies, perhaps, a return from those heights on which no man may permanently live to this less real but more insistent world in which we are plunged in the last movement, a world where heroism which is also pathetic marches to its end attended by yearning and pain. It may or it may not be of symbolic significance that Beethoven makes some use of the fugue theme in this last movement. But the character of the theme, as it occurs here, is entirely changed, and any symbolic significance it may have is not obvious.

The final quartet, whether by coincidence or design, is in the same key as the very first, F Major. Completed if not wholly written at Gneixendorf, it bespeaks Beethoven's sense of inner release (however outwardly he may have gone on fighting) at the deliverance of his nephew and himself from subjugating love. It also bespeaks a recognition that he has said what he wanted to say in the three preceding works. He now proposes, rather than repeat himself or pile Ossa on Pelion, to return to an almost Mozartean delicacy of treatment. There are four movements again (the C-sharp Minor had seven), a properly "balanced" sequence of force, wit, gravity and release that the eighteenth century artist would not have dreamed of violating. Everything—except in the slow movement (to describe any movement in the C-sharp Minor as either "slow" or "fast" would be to deny its integrated character)—is clipped, precise, almost dry. Almost—because a rapier-like probing, close to surgical in delight with which it seems to puncture all pretentious excrescences, informs every measure of this reflective postscript. The *Vivace* is a ghostly reprise of mammoth symphonic scherzos, a macabre syncopation of *calaveras*. The slow movement is a worthy sister of the heartbreaking *Cavatina* of the B-flat Quartet, but without the anguish—"Beklemmt" Beethoven had written over that world's dirge. The finale is a wacky dialogue, grim only for a split second now and then, on the *"Muss es sein?" "Es muss sein!"* exchange that took place one day, according to Schindler, between Beethoven and a housekeeper who asked for shopping-money. "Must it be?" Beethoven asked, to which she replied with finality, "It must be!" Grave commentators, looking for a last colloquy with Fate, have brushed the explanation aside as unspeakably trivial.

I'll go along with Schindler. "To see the world in a grain of sand," said another great mystic whose feet remained as firmly planted in this earth. Only the squeamish, or those who link reverence with denial, are surprised that Beethoven could turn from the religious involvements of the Mass in D to write a friend "I wish you open bowels and a handsome and convenient stool." And only an analyst lacking in humor could interpret this and similar ribald utterances to indicate psychic ill health. For a good many years the last quartets, with their angular rhythms, dissonant harmonies, and substitution of expressive for conventional architecture, were widely regarded as signifying the composer's senility if not his madness. Even Joseph de Marliave, French author of an exhaustive treatise on the quartets, goes to absurd lengths to present Beethoven as all-noble, the innocent victim of false friends and wicked relatives, apparently in an effort to establish the "sanity" of the late works. Never had Beethoven written with more economy than in the F Major Quartet and never with more creative health than in his next (and final) composition, the rollicking second-ending to the B-flat. There is every reason to suppose that had Beethoven lived another ten or twenty years he would have given the world still more reasons—as only Shakespeare so completely had—to justify its often dubious claims to sanity:

> *I am but mad north-northwest: when the wind is southerly*
> *I know a hawk from a handsaw. . . .*

"DISEMBODIED, TRIUMPHANT"

O Goethe! [wrote Bettina in a letter to the poet] No prince or emperor ever felt conscious like Beethoven of the reality of his omnipotence, and the sense that he is the source of all strength and power. He stood there, erect, with an indomitable force flowing from him. . . . His genius seemed to transform everything into a deliberate and conscious activity.

. . . One felt that a day must come when, in a new and perfect existence, he would reappear as the Lord of the world.

Bettina in her "raptus" after seeing and hearing Beethoven conduct one of his symphonies, came close to the truth. "Activity" is the operative word. Unless we are seized by it and communicate it others, what are we? "I am electrical," said Beethoven in a "raptus" of his own to Bettina, and the awareness of this rare and necessary state of being was to be the burden of a poem by that artist in America who came closest, though not very close, to being a Beethoven. As he lay dying Walt Whitman made his peace with Death in the sense that Beethoven had, almost from the beginning:

> *Who touches this touches a man. . . .*
> *Remember my words, I may return again.*
> *I love you, I depart from materials.*
> *I am as one disembodied, triumphant, dead. . . .*
> *Shunning postponing severance,*
> *Seeking to ward off the last word ever so little. . . .*
> *Loath, O so loath to depart!*
> *Garrulous to the very last.*

Let us take leave, then, of him in whose music death has no place, propped in that dirty bed reading Handel, talking to "Trouser Button" or anyone else who happens by, grousing with the servants and doctors out of force of habit, and no doubt with the priest, and certainly with those busybody but withal loveable secretaries. Talking so much, unquestionably, because aware that there isn't time to bring any more noteworthy (how Beethoven loved those bad puns!) discourse to a finish; and what is worth doing, one can hear him ask, that is not worth finishing? He looks at the row of bells on the table but doesn't pick them up to test his ear this time; it is too late for that. The fire that brought down the bell-tower, that later on burnt out the world of princely possessions and unworthy gratuities, has finally reached the flesh, but cannot stop that immortal ringing or even this time-defying talk! The heart, and only the heart, survives.

Appendixes

1. AUTHOR'S NOTE

The inspiration of what I have called Beethoven's 'unblindered optimism' has been a central and guiding experience in my life. At every turn the recognition has coincided with events outside and within, leading finally—and not without humility —to the rashness of this undertaking. In my 'twenties I shared the feeling about Beethoven with a friend who expressed it for himself in his own inimitable fashion:

> I will tell you a test. It is untrue. It stacks all the cards. It is out of line with what the composer intended. All so much the better.
>
> Get a radio or a phonograph capable of the most extreme loudness possible and sit down and listen to a performance of Beethoven's Seventh Symphony. . . . If it hurts you, be glad of it. As near as you will ever get, you are inside the music; not only inside it, you are it; your body is no longer your shape and substance, it is the shape and substance of the music.
>
> Is what you hear pretty? or beautiful? or legal? or acceptable in polite or any other society? It is beyond any calculation savage and dangerous and murderous to all equilibrium in human life as human life is; and nothing can equal the rape it does on all that death; nothing except anything, anything in existence or dream, perceived anywhere remotely toward its true dimension.
>
> Beethoven said a thing as rash and noble as the best of his work. By my memory, he said: "He who understands my music can never know unhappiness again." I believe it.
>
> —James Agee in *Let Us Now Praise Famous Men,* 1939

As an adolescent, I had divorced myself from "music" as I then grasped its meaning. That meaning was formed from what I heard of the piano instructions given my sister by a close friend of my mother. This celebrated teacher had studied with Liszt, who in turn had played for Beethoven. Her pupils were graduated from the scales to Czerny, and from there to Hummel, Moszkowski, and Grieg (if they showed rewarding diligence). At times the sonatas of Clementi, Haydn, and Mozart were played as if they belonged in the same uninspired company. I refused—and regretted it later, of course—to become a part of this by studying the piano.

My eighteenth year found me in a house containing an ancient player-piano. Convinced of my immunity to becoming tainted by the music I had so narrowly escaped, I sometimes played one of the many recordings piled high in the closet. "Butterflies," "Spinning Wheel" and "Lovedream" fluttered from the keys, making little impression, until one day a fat spool labeled "Sonate Pathétique" began to unroll.

Those rebellious opening chords fell upon me like blows. The shell of my sullen resistance began to crumble. The grave movement that followed the first, *cantabile,* was a love song of unabashed sentiment but somehow given dignity by the fiercely masculine statements enclosing it. The concluding Rondo soared as no verbally-invoked Skylark could ever hope to. Enthralled as I was already by the Romantic poets, here was Byron, Keats, Shelley, rolled into one. If this was what young Werther had been trying to say in those interminable monologues the young liberator Napoleon carried with him on the battlefields—why had he never said it? The economy of Beethoven's proclamation, its decisiveness, had lost nothing in the passage of time. Even the deathless ardor of Romeo at the tomb, projected with as much poetry, was fighting a losing battle with "paramours" and "apothecaries."

During a year in Germany, then poised on the brink of the most terrible rejection of humanity the world was ever to witness, I came closer to understanding the Second Period "duel" between convulsion and order in Beethoven's music. Innocence (the cynical who have the benefit of hindsight would call it naiveté) was as prevalent in the Berlin of 1932 as it had been before the French Revolution's Reign of Terror in Beethoven's time. Hopes were as high. Disaster was as imminent. Idealists in their flight from the accepted, unromantic safeguards of the existing order—the survival of which alone guaranteed them the freedom to agitate—

144

flocked to the Red or Brown standards of revolution. They reviled each other passionately over differences that were minimal, but agreed upon the necessity of "temporarily" sacrificing the right of every dissenter but themselves to be heard.

Lovers of Beethoven were to be found in both camps. A sixteen-year-old girl, an innocent humanitarian, was in the process of converting her whole family to Hitler. Her parents must sacrifice their personal freedom for the sake of Germany's greater need, she said. I remember watching her dissolve in tears when she heard the last movement of the "Waldstein" Sonata. When I asked her what sanction for the sadism of her comrades she found in it, she replied that the house must be purified before its inmates could deserve such spirituality. A Communist music-lover I knew never tired of quoting Maxim Gorky's story of Lenin listening privately while an eminent pianist played him the "Appassionata." "It affects my nerves," Lenin had said, "and makes me want to say sweet nothings and stroke the heads of men who live in a dirty hell and still create such beauty. But these days you can't go around stroking people's heads lest your hand be bitten off. You have to smash them over the head—smash them without mercy. . . ."

In the years of exhaustion following the war, I listened with a growing comprehension to the music Beethoven finally wrote, the music of his Third Period. Why was the typical artist of our time willing to settle for so much less? In the visual and auditory arts any attempt to come to grips with the great human issues, as Beethoven had done—issues for which ordinary men were fighting and dying—had long since been ruled out.

Yet rules in art exist to be broken. And how many "typical" artists are ever remembered? Had the Schools of Paris and New York become academies? The contemporary period was beginning to produce non-conformists. And their morally committed, communicable expression was repeating Beethoven's creative journey in at least one respect. Invention as an end in itself was disdained. The new works were organically related to the great tradition; in the course of their unfolding, tribute was paid to the masters of ages past. Orozco, at the very outset of his career, dared to build on Masaccio. Toward the end, though speaking in his unique style, he paid homage to El Greco. Standing under the dome of the *Hospicio* at Guadalajara, one could think of Beethoven on his deathbed reading with exultant disbelief from the forty volumes of the scores of Handel.

145

The growing company of adventurous spirits who followed Orozco and dared to pit their fury and compassion with the masters' had other characteristics in common. They dared to be falsely accused of moving backward. They dared to be crucified by the critics for spurning "beauty." They dared to be read. They dared to trace the ravages of pride or contrition on a human face. They dared to move beyond the hermetic confines of the creative ego. "The artist," Beethoven once wrote a littl girl, "has no pride, he unfortunately sees that art has no limits; he feels darkly how far away he is from the goal; and though he may be admired by others, he grieves not yet to have come there, to where his better genius lights him only as a distant sun."

2. THE ARTIST

From such a master as Beethoven every epoch, through its own revaluation, must try to profit. Since our society has witnessed the virtual abdication of will in human affairs, its arts have reflected that paralysis, with little emphasis on tragic commitment, human content, or even meaning. To encourage the revival of art forms as ambitious and demanding as Beethoven's, by focusing on the close connection between this artist's music and his life-experience, was half my purpose.

The other (and closely related) half was to provide an appropriate vehicle

146

for a living artist in whose work I had limitless faith, an artist who seemed capable of interpreting what never had been attempted pictorially. Beethoven while he lived was sketched, drawn, caricatured, painted, sculptured, life-masked, and death-masked by a swarm of artisans, but he never encountered an artist. Goya alone, of those living at the time, could have done him justice. Among contemporary artists of stature, James Kearns seemed as well prepared to do so as any. The tragic in Kearns' hands never wanted nobility, and he was a tragic artist first; indignation over human degradation and waste (which no committed artist in our age can possibly avoid expressing) never in Kearns' imagery exhibited a trace of perverse exultation or meanness. I hope I have indicated that humor—as opposed to wit— is one of the basic ingredients of Beethoven's work and one in which it towers over that of any other composer. The same *kind* of humor was to be found in Kearns. Where earthy responses were called for—boisterous, satiric, corrosive, scorching— they were at his command. His capacity for portraiture, compassionate as well as penetrating, yielded to none.

3. SOURCES

In his essay on Moses as a great "father image," inspiring fear as well as devotion, Freud mentions three artists—Leonardo da Vinci, Goethe, and Beethoven—whose personalities over and above their work have impressed themselves on mankind. Freud chose to devote a pathographical study to Leonardo, about whose life very little is known. Goethe wrote so much about himself, and labored so persistently

to "create" the kind of personality he wished to be known by, that the "truth" will probably never be known. Beethoven concealed nothing, either in his music or in the records he left of his life. And the records are more voluminous than those documenting any major artist in history. There were, at last count, 1580 surviving letters. Of the 400 Conversation Books recording the "talk" during the years of deafness, 136 survived—until their mysterious disappearance behind the Iron Curtain following World War II. Substantial portions of the 136 have appeared in French and German translation, and of course all of them were accessible to Thayer and the later biographers.

The Life of Ludwig van Beethoven by Alexander Wheelock Thayer (ed. Deiters, Riemann, & Krehbiel, 3 vols., New York, 1921) is the standard source book of all studies of Beethoven, and has been mine. One does not read Thayer for character-analysis or musical interpretation and the two biographies that best supply these deficiencies are John N. Burk's *The Life and Works of Beethoven* (New York, 1943) and Marion M. Scott's *Beethoven* (London, 1934). From these three works, from *Beethoven's Letters* (ed. Lady Wallace, 2 vols., London, 1866),[1] from *Beethoven's Letters, Journals and Conversations* (ed. Michael Hamburger, New York, 1960) and from *Beethoven and His Nephew: A Psychoanalytic Study of Their Relationship* by Editha and Richard Sterba, M.D. I have drawn all quotations not otherwise identified in the text. For the two most illuminating essays on the music, Donald Francis Tovey's *Beethoven* (London, 1944) and J. W. N. Sullivan's *Beethoven: His Spiritual Development* (London, 1927), every lover of Beethoven must be grateful.

The quotation from Haydn's letter about Beethoven is from the former's *Collected Correspondence and London Notebooks* (ed. H. C. Robbins Landon, New York, 1960). The quotations from Paul Henry Lang are from his monumental *Music in Western Civilization* (New York, 1941) and from his weekly music criticism in the New York *Herald Tribune*. The quotations from Bernard Shaw are from *Shaw on Music* (ed. Eric Bentley, New York, 1955). The quotations from Dana Steichen are from her *Beethoven's Beloved* (New York, 1959). Ernest Newman's remarks on the Missa Solemnis are from his notes to the RCA Victor recording.

[1] Emily Anderson's definitive three-volume edition of the letters was published late in 1961 after the completion of the present book.

Richard Wagner's comments on the Ninth Symphony are from his autobiography, *My Life* (London, 1911). The quotation from Karl Pidoll is from his novel, *Eroica* (New York, 1956). The quotations from Michelangelo are from *Le Rime di Michelangelo Buonarotti* (Firenze, 1863) and the translations are taken from Joseph Tusiani's *The Complete Poems of Michelangelo* (New York, 1960). Spohr's observations on Beethoven are from *The Musical Journeys of Louis Spohr* (ed. Henry Pleasants, Norman, Oklahoma, 1961). Bettina von Arnim's description of Beethoven conducting is from Goethe's *Briefwechsel mit einem Kinde* as translated in Joseph de Marliave's *Beethoven's Quartets* (New York, 1961).

4. DISCOGRAPHY

Almost all the music Beethoven wrote is available on LP records, much of it in a half-dozen or more different performances. The selected list which follows is only for the convenience of those readers unfamiliar with what is available. It includes the compositions mentioned in the text in the recordings familiar to the author and is arranged in Beethoven's three "periods" as defined in the text.

Opus Number	Composition	LP Recording
	FIRST PERIOD	
1	Three Trios (E-flat, G, C Minor) for Piano, Violin & Violoncello	No. 1 Columbia ML 5291 (Casals, Fuchs, Istomin) No. 3 Westminster 18030 (Fournier, Janigro, Badura-Skoda)
2	Three Piano Sonatas (F Minor, A, C)	London LL949,948, 627 (Backhaus)
10	Three Piano Sonatas (C Minor, F, D)	No. 3 Decca 9584 (Kempff)
13	Piano Sonata in C Minor (*Pathétique*)	Victor LM 1908 (Rubinstein)
14	Two Piano Sonatas (E, G)	No. 2 Decca 9592 (Kempff)
15	Piano Concerto in C	Vic. LM 2120 (Rubinstein)
18	Six String Quartets (F, G, D, C Minor, A, B-flat)	3-Col. SL-172 (Budapest)
26	Piano Sonata in A-flat	Decca 9589 (Kempff)
27	Two Piano Sonatas *Quasi una Fantasia*, No. 1 in E-flat, No. 2 in C-sharp Minor ("Moonlight")	Decca 9584, 9582 (Kempff)
31	Three Piano Sonatas (G, D Minor, E-flat)	Nos. 2 & 3 Angel 35352 (Gieseking)
36	Symphony Number Two in D	Vic. LM 1723 (Toscanini)

Opus Number	Composition	LP Recording
	SECOND PERIOD	
54	Symphony Number Three in E-flat ("Eroica")	Col. ML 5320 (Walther)
53	Piano Sonata in C ("Waldstein")	West. 18086 (Lateiner)
57	Piano Sonata in F Minor ("Appassionata")	Vic. LM 1908 (Rubinstein)
58	Piano Concerto in G	Col. ML 5037 (Serkin)
59	Three String Quartets in F, E Minor, C ("Rasoumovsky")	Col. ML 4579, 4580, 4581 (Budapest)
60	Symphony Number Four in B-flat	Vic. LM 1757 (Toscanini)
61	Violin Concerto in D	Angel 35780 (Oistrakh)
67	Symphony Number Five in C Minor	Vic. LM 1757 (Toscanini)
69	Sonata for Violoncello in A	Col. ML 3878 (Casals, Serkin)
70	Two Trios for Piano, Violin, Violoncello in D and E-flat	No. 1 Col. ML 5291 (Casals, Fuchs, Istomin) No. 2 Col. ML 4571 Casals, Schneider, Istomin)
72	*Fidelio* (Opera in Two Acts)	2-Vic. LM 6025 (Toscanini)
72a	Overture "Leonora Number Three"	Angel 35097 (Von Karajan)
73	Piano Concerto in E-flat ("Emperor")	Col. ML 4623 (Gieseking)
74	String Quartet in E-flat ("Harp")	Col. ML 4582 (Budapest)
78	Piano Sonata in F-sharp	Decca 9578 (Kempff)
81a	Piano Sonata in E-flat (*Lebewohl*)	London LM 9085 (Backhaus)
84	Overture to *Egmont*	Angel 35097 (Von Karajan)
86	Mass in C	Cap. SG 7168 (Beecham)
90	Piano Sonata in E Minor	London LM 9085 (Backhaus)
91	Wellington's Victory ("Battle of Vittoria")	Oc. 34 (Leibowitz)
92	Symphony Number Seven in A	Vic. LM 1756 (Toscanini)
93	Symphony Number Eight in F	Vic. LM 1757 (Toscanini)
95	String Quartet in F Minor (*Serioso*)	Col. ML 4581 (Budapest)
96	Violin Sonata in G	Vic. LM 1914 (Heifetz)
97	Trio in B-flat ("Archduke")	Col. ML 4574 (Casals, Istomin, Schneider)
98	Song Cycle (*An die ferne Geliebte*)	Electra 90052 (Fischer-Dieskau)
	THIRD PERIOD	
101	Piano Sonata in A	Decca 9581 (Kempff)
102	Two Violoncello Sonatas in C and D	Col. ML 4876, 4878 (Casals, Serkin)
106	Piano Sonata in B-flat (*Hammerklavier*)	Decca 9579 (Kempff)

Opus Number	Composition	LP Recording
111	Piano Sonata in C Minor	Decca 9587 (Kempff)
120	Thirty-three Variations for the Piano (in C) on a Waltz by Diabelli	Col. ML 5246 (Serkin)
123	*Missa Solemnis* (Mass) in D for Orchestra, Chorus & Four Solo Voices	2-Vic. LM6013 (Toscanini) 2-Col. M2L 270 (Bernstein)
125	Symphony Number Nine in D Minor ("Choral")	2-Vic. LM 6009 (Toscanini)
126	Six Bagatelles (and all earlier ones)	Van. 1033 (Matthews)
127	String Quartet in E-flat	Col. ML 4583 (Budapest)
132	String Quartet in A Minor	Col. ML 4586 (Budapest)
130	String Quartet in B-flat	Col. ML 4584 (Budapest)
133	*Grosse Fugue* in B-flat (for String Quartet)	Col. ML 4587 (Budapest)
131	String Quartet in C-sharp Minor	Col. ML 5485 (Budapest)
135	String Quartet in F	Col. ML 4587 (Budapest)

INDEX

of persons, not including the composer
and his family, referred to in the text

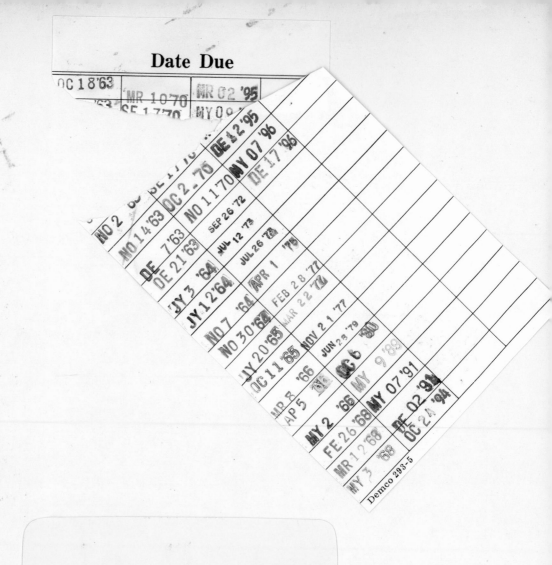